APACHE SUNRISE

MEMORIES FROM SAN CARLOS

SONJA WHITE DAVID

FOREWORD BY JOEL NILSSON

THE History PRESS

Published by The History Press
Charleston, SC 29403
www.historypress.net

First published 2015

Manufactured in the United States

ISBN 978.1.62619.861.6

Library of Congress Control Number: 2014955128

Notice: The information in this book is true and complete to the best of our knowledge. It is offered without guarantee on the part of the author or The History Press. The author and The History Press disclaim all liability in connection with the use of this book.

APACHE SUNRISE

To Richard, and to our children, Patrick, Christopher, Noelle and Holly, each one born right before we arrived at one reservation or soon after we left another; to the memory of my mother, Patti, who loved to visit San Carlos; and to the people of the San Carlos Reservation. I hold you all in my heart with love.

Contents

Foreword

Life is a series of peaks and valleys. The rhythms of day-to-day life on a Native American reservation, the ups and downs, the joys and sorrows, are vividly pictured through the splendid window that Sonja David graciously has opened.

Sonja's engaging memoir chronicles the five years that she and her husband, Richard, lived on the San Carlos Indian Reservation, about ninety miles east of Phoenix. They were, she says, the happiest years of her life. Told with beautiful sensitivity, grace and profound compassion, her memoir, *Apache Sunrise: Memories from San Carlos*, is a seminal journey of self-discovery and a delightful reminiscence of living in a culture that few Anglos know. Through her everyday cross-cultural living experiences, Sonja's penchant for greater understanding of Apache traditions grew and grew, so much so that when the time came to leave she had a difficult time saying farewell.

Not many people have heard of San Carlos, one of the most isolated and poorest Indian reservations in America, where the unemployment rate is at all times over 50 percent and health problems are wide-ranging and grave. For those who have heard of San Carlos, it likely is in conjunction with the Apache leader Geronimo, who, with his small band of warriors, bedeviled and outwitted the U.S. Cavalry for twelve years after the San Carlos Reservation was created. Accounts of the day described San Carlos as horrible, a place more habitable for rattlesnakes and Gila monsters than people.

My introduction to San Carlos was through Sonja's husband, Richard. At the time, I was a reporter for the *Arizona Daily Star*, the morning newspaper in

Tucson. It was late one fall afternoon, and I, fresh out of graduate school, had worked at the newspaper for only a couple of weeks. The managing editor, Frank Johnson, walked out of his glass-enclosed office, looked around the newsroom and saw that I was not busy. He instructed me to talk with the two guests being led into the newsroom and to determine if there was a story.

Richard introduced himself as a Bureau of Indian Affairs employment specialist from San Carlos. With him was a handsome fourteen-year-old Apache youth by the name of Eldad Goode who had shoulder-length hair. Not a hippie of the 1970s, he was just a reservation kid who had good grades and a fine attendance record in elementary school and who wanted to wear his locks as his ancestors had as he began high school.

It didn't take long for Globe High School to suspend Eldad because his hair length did not conform to the school's dress code. Richard thought this was a classic case of discrimination and a violation of his due process as guaranteed by the Fourteenth Amendment to the U.S. Constitution. I went to Globe to interview school officials and wrote the story. It took several weeks, but a restraining order finally was issued.

For Richard and Sonja, this activism relit the fires of their peaceful demonstrations in Chicago and their involvement with the Reverend Jesse Jackson's Operation Breadbasket. Richard and Eldad planned to deliver the restraining order to the principal. Sonja wanted to go, too, and her memoir relives the incident with colorful description and indignation, followed by internal questioning of whether they should have interfered.

> *The autumn air was warm and hazy…As we walked up the impossibly steep flight of broad stone steps, I wondered if he felt as nervous as I did. My hands were cold and wet and my stomach lurched, and all I had to do was watch while Eldad took the heat. I'd never felt this frightened marching down State Street, not even in front of the Chicago Police…*
>
> *The principal turned in his swivel chair to face us.* Why, he actually has a red neck! *I thought, startled…The principal stared at the piece of paper* [and] *glared at Richard.*
>
> *"Get to class. Boy." The principal waved us away and began shuffling papers on his desk.*
>
> *I opened my mouth, but I saw Richard's warning glance. I compressed my lips and did not call the principal a jerk.*
>
> *The passing bell rang as we left the office and the hall filled quickly with chattering, yelling students who suddenly turned silent the instant they saw Eldad.*

> *As he walked toward his locker alone he looked like a shy, small bird that stumbled into a nest of vultures.* Oh, God, *I thought, my stomach tightening,* maybe we shouldn't have interfered! *What if things went harder on him now than if he* had *cut off his hair? Maybe these kids hated Apaches as much as generations of Globe residents before them.*

Sonja tells her story with passion and compassion. Her observations sparkle. Her sensitivity explodes off the page. The reader is carried along by Sonja's lively prose that captures the importance of tribal elder Clarence Wesley; the beautiful guitar music of Chiliboy; tensions between the Davids and Sister Conquistadora, a Catholic nun who wasn't happy with her assignment at San Carlos; the healing powers of faith; the humor of trying to learn to speak the Apache language. Her experiences are a kaleidoscope of heartfelt emotions that resonate and instruct.

Sonja is at her absolute best in detailing her reverence for the Apache culture, the blending of the physical and spiritual worlds that lifted away her initial feelings of restlessness and led her to be comfortable and to appreciate the Apache ways.

These meaningful years, working in near oblivion, are some of Sonja and Richard's most cherished moments. I understand why these years have a special place in their hearts. I served in the Peace Corps in a distant land and came to grips with a different culture. Cross-cultural experiences lead to better understanding and personal enrichment, and so it is with Richard and Sonja.

Joel Nilsson
Retired editorial writer and editorial board member of the *Arizona Republic*
Phoenix, Arizona

Preface

In writing this memoir, it was necessary to read dozens of letters from our San Carlos Apache friends and thousands of pages of journal notes and draft chapters dating back forty years. Consistently, the words caused teary eyes and a longing to board a time machine back to the first five years of the 1970s. Paradoxically, even though the San Carlos Apache Reservation with its 60 percent unemployment rate was one of the poorest in America, it was my experience that humor, wisdom, patience and hope were deployed against pervasive malevolence and that they regularly won the day, just as Geronimo's guerrilla tactics had done so often in his time. As I assembled notes and began writing recollections, I felt both sadness and joy. The crushing poverty imposed on the Apache people notwithstanding, I chose to write this book by the lights the San Carlos people shone into even the darkest areas of life itself.

Acknowledgements

My thanks:

to Harold Winters of the Tattered Cover Book Store in Denver who brought my manuscript to the attention of Miki Atencio of The History Press and to John Lake, dear friend of many years who introduced me to Miki, first by e-mail and then in person at that beautiful dinner party;

to Christen Thompson, senior editor at The History Press, for her enthusiasm and encouragement;

to Joel Nilsson, who as a young reporter for the *Arizona Daily Star* knew a good story when he saw one;

to Monica Boni, old school friend of Patrick and Christopher at St. Charles, who brought Richard and me together with Chiliboy after forty years;

to Herb Stevens, director of the San Carlos Apache Cultural Center, for so much help and good advice;

to Richard, whose photographs illuminate my words. All photographs, unless otherwise credited, are his.

Ahi' yi' ee

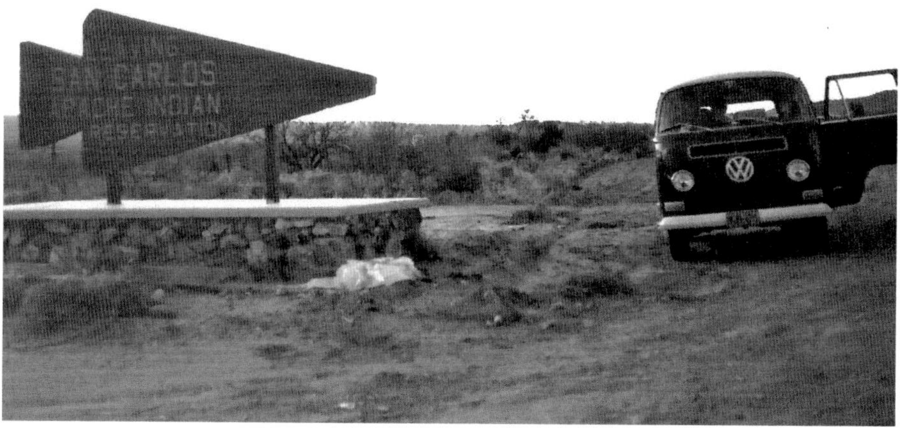

In early May 1975, before the dawn, we left San Carlos forever.

Prologue

Arizona Republic, *November 14, 21, 2013*
Copper-mine bill stalls in House

Plans to build North America's largest copper mine near Superior were dealt a major blow Wednesday when congressional supporters of the project canceled a vote on their bill after a strong lobbying effort against the mine by Native American tribes throughout the nation.

The San Carlos Apache Tribe, which fears the mine will destroy its sacred land, reached out to tribes across the country for help in stopping the project.

Opponents of the mine say it would weaken the ground beneath sacred Native American lands such as Apache Leap, harm the environment and rock-climbing areas, and threaten the Phoenix area's water supply.

The bill prohibits…mining…beneath Apache Leap, a sacred tribal site where legend has it that Apache warriors leaped off a cliff rather than surrender to federal troops in the 1870s. However, tribal leaders say that mining would harm the entire area, including Apache Leap.

Terry Rambler, chairman of the San Carlos Apache Tribe, said he believes the underground mine will cause sacred tribal lands above it to weaken, creating sinkholes and troughs.

Rambler said the Oak Flat area is the site of ceremonial tribal rituals, including the sunrise ceremony, which celebrates a young woman's coming of age.

> *"This area is like Mount Sinai to us," Rambler said, referring to the Biblical site where Moses received the Ten Commandments. "It* [the land exchange] *will destroy our sacred area."*

Erin Kelly's feature articles took me back nearly forty years to my own sacred site—a place I had come to know as holy—and the day I had to leave it forever.

On May 10, 1975, somewhere between Springerville, Arizona, and Red Hill, New Mexico, something broke inside me. I fell asleep and the red Volkswagen bus I was driving drifted over the line, across the left lane of U.S. Route 60 and smack into the high desert.

"Just slithered across the highway like a lizard," said Richard, who'd been driving up ahead and looking out for me in the rearview mirror. "You scared the hell out of me! Why didn't you just pull over if you were getting sleepy?"

"I don't remember getting sleepy," I told him. One minute I'd been looking ahead, watching the brown and white ears of Joshua, our St. Bernard, his knobby head bobbing up and down in the rear window of the old gray Renault, thinking how funny the big dog looked in the little car, and the next minute I was barreling through scrub oak.

"Mama!" Noelle had screamed. I'd jammed my foot on the brake. "Mama!" my five-year-old daughter screamed again. My ten-year-old son, Patrick, glared at me, his wire-rimmed glasses dangling on the tip of his nose. "What did you do that for?" He pushed his glasses back up on his face. "What *happened*?"

"What happened?" Richard echoed. He had stopped his car and run to the bus, followed by eight-year-old Christopher and the barking dog, sending the cat, Mary Ann, who'd been riding next to me, skittering behind the back seat.

"I don't know," I said, my voice as shaky as my hands. "Boy, I really do not want to leave the reservation, do I?

"You shouldn't be leaving," the Apache man had said to us a few hours earlier when we'd stopped at the rest area in Salt River Canyon just before crossing from the San Carlos Reservation into Whiteriver. "Why you leaving?" He threw his arms around my husband.

"Well, I guess it's just time to move on," Richard said, disentangling himself and giving the man a pat on the back. The man watched us mournfully as we headed back to our cars.

"Your place is here with us, Mister," the man shouted suddenly. "Here with *us*."

I stopped and stared back at the man. "Who is he?" I asked, struck with a wild, irrational hope that this Indian had been sent to give me a last-minute reprieve.

"I don't know," Richard said. "I honestly don't. I've never seen him before in my life."

"But how does he *know*?"

He shook his head. "How do they all know? They just do. You know that."

I did know that. Sometimes they knew secret things, the Apaches, in non-empirical ways.

They knew I was pregnant.

"For you, Sonja," Agnes had said night before last. "A going away gift." She'd giggled while the women at the Catholic mission gently placed a beaded Apache cradle board into my arms.

How did they know? I'd wondered, blinking back tears, as the ladies, their long, bright camp dresses fluttering, hovered over me possessively. I was only eight weeks along, and Richard and I hadn't told our own mothers yet or even our three children.

"Now, if you get the least little bit drowsy again, honk the horn and pull over," Richard said as he poured me another cup of coffee. "We can take our time. We don't have to be in Denver before next Monday."

Why did we have to be in Denver at all?

"I hope you will be happy up there in that cold weather," Buck Kitcheyan, the tribal chairman, had told us only last night. "Maybe you will freeze." A hundred or more of us stood silently in a grove of cottonwood trees down by the San Carlos River as the chairman dipped his thumb into a small buckskin bag and marked a cross of yellow pollen on my husband's forehead and the palms of his hands.

"What does it do, this ceremony?" Richard turned the buckskin bag around in his hand and looked at it, carefully, as the two of them stood in the glow of the bonfire.

"It makes you homesick," the chairman said. He laughed. "It makes you want to come back to us."

I want to go back *now*, I thought, sadly, as I put the bus in gear and headed east. Five years ago, who'd have believed it?

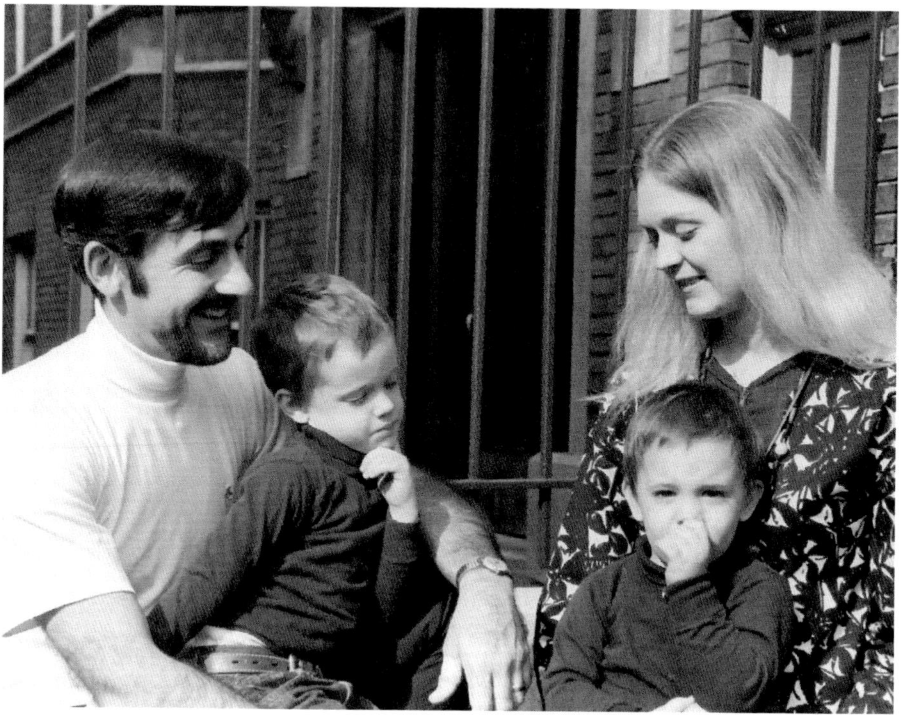

Chicago, 1968: Richard, Patrick, Christopher and I are in front of our apartment building.
Photo by Deck McLean.

Bright Morning

It's blue!"

Our four-year-old son, Patrick, stared at the sky. Our airplane had just broken through the clouds after leaving Chicago's O'Hare Airport. It was spring of 1969, and we were on vacation and going home to Arizona.

"What color do you think the sky is supposed to be, Pat?" Richard asked.

"Gray."

Richard and I looked at each other. Gray? Of course. The way he saw it in Chicago, where we had lived since 1966, when Richard had been transferred to the Chicago Field Office of the Bureau of Indian Affairs. That incident in the airplane reminded Richard and me that we were desert rats who had grown up taking blue sky and sunshine for granted.

But in spite of the gray skies and cold weather, Richard and I loved Chicago; it was light years removed from our small hometown of Chandler, Arizona, and it provided experiences that made us feel sophisticated and liberated.

At Pequeo's, a restaurant on the North Side, we ate (the owner swore to it) five-hundred-year-old potatoes from a volcano in Peru. Along with our friends John and Terri McCarthy, we became such regular customers that we were the only North Americans invited to Pequeo's first anniversary celebration. Emboldened by a steady stream of red wine and cheered on by dozens of clapping Peruvians, we danced stuff we'd never done in our lives: tangos, rumbas and sambas.

Dance makes a good metaphor for our liberation. While I danced in ways I had never dreamed of, Richard danced for the first time ever. Urged on by our friend Calvin Morris, Richard gyrated, hipped and hopped as if he'd been born to it. And we discovered the ballet—from the traditional *Swan Lake* by the Soviet Union's Bolshoi, to its recent defector, Rudolf Nureyev, who stunned the audience by diving, in a crashing finale, through a paper backdrop of giant red lips. While a few members of the audience walked out of the theater in protest, Richard and I remained to watch Nureyev dance once more with his partner, Dame Margot Fonteyn, and, at the end, kneel and kiss her hand.

And there were the museums. Our boys loved the Museum of Science and Industry, which they called the button museum because there were so many of them to push. One button crashed a wrecking ball on a chain into a wall of Plexiglas that never broke. Another caused pieces of Samsonite luggage to bang around against each other and not be damaged. There was a real submarine to explore, as well as a replica of a beating human heart, tall enough for an adult to walk through. On the outside of the giant heart, coronary arteries would light up in sequence as the blood flowed through the four chambers.

One day at the Chicago Art Institute, I wandered by accident into a narrow room and looked up to see, filling an entire two-story wall, El Greco's *Assumption of the Virgin*, a small print of which had hung high on the wall at the north end of another two-story room, the vast study hall of Chandler High School. The study hall had been cooled only by a small circulating fan, and for endless hours (dripping with sweat from the five crinoline petticoats beneath my vast poodle skirt) I'd escaped both boredom and the blistering heat of May by gazing up at that picture and imagining myself ascending, like Mary, into the stratosphere. Encountering the real thing and finding it hundreds of times larger than my high school icon dazzled me.

How many other surprises were out there waiting to be discovered?

Politics, for one. We were Democrats, but we'd never done anything political other than vote. That changed when we moved to Chicago's South Side. The mix of people in our South Shore neighborhood generated political action, and we were ready. I've thought over the years how different our lives would have been had we settled, say, on the North Side or in one of the suburbs. I would never have met Pam McLean and her little son, Bradley, in the park down the street, nor would Richard have gone with Pam's husband, Deck (a reporter for *Ebony* magazine), to Grant Park to observe the demonstrations at the 1968 Democratic National Convention. We would never have known the African American Episcopal priest Bill Wetzel, who introduced us to Jesse Jackson's Operation Breadbasket, which we attended on Saturdays; would never have become such good friends with Jesse's assistant, the Reverend Calvin Morris, and his wife, Judith. Now we marched in civil rights and peace demonstrations. One of our younger son Christopher's earliest memories is of holding a sign and being pushed in his stroller around and around in front of a Walgreens Drugstore not far from our South Shore apartment building. That particular picket line went on for twelve weeks before Walgreens signed a "covenant" with Operation Breadbasket, promising to hire black managers in black neighborhoods.

Demonstrating, we learned, need not be confined to the streets. Father Bill Wetzel had, upon his ordination, been assigned to our parish, St. Margaret's Episcopal Church in South Shore. After a few months, it became obvious Bill was given only subservient roles. He rarely, for example, was assigned to preach a sermon. In other words, he was the token African American (other than the janitor) on the staff. Bill was responsible for the youth group, and he asked us to help him chaperone the dances the youth group sponsored in the church basement on Saturday nights. The dances, which featured live local bands, drew huge crowds, and one of the duties Richard and I were assigned was to check the restrooms for anyone smoking pot.

"Smoking marijuana?" I said. "How are we supposed to know that?"

"Easy," Bill assured us. "It smells like perfume."

Perfume? What on earth did he mean? Nothing in that restroom resembled any perfume I had ever smelled. Richard and I were such terrible narcs that Bill himself took on that duty and posted us at different spots at the edge of the dance floor to "keep things in hand." It seemed to us things were getting out of hand when, in the last dance one night, the lead player smashed his guitar to smithereens. The crowd loved it.

Although the youth group had only seven or eight members, they were active. They picked up trash from public areas and planted trees along the edges of South Shore Drive. They raised funds by shoveling snow, cleaning up yards and babysitting, and they gave the money to Father Peter Powell at St. Augustine's Indian Center, which was affiliated with the Episcopal Church. And they liked to protest. They loved their young priest, Father Bill, and they took it as a personal affront that they never got to hear him preach. They decided they would demonstrate their anger in church, and we agreed to help them. One Sunday morning, we all sat in the back of the church and at one point in the service we stood up and, accompanied by John Wilkinson on his guitar, sang "We Shall Overcome" as loudly as we could. We sang as many verses as we could think of, and when we finished those, we went back to the beginning and sang some more. The rector and the choir, looking embarrassed, silently filed out through the side door next to the altar.

None of this, of course, had any effect, except to make us feel good. Bill was still not allowed to preach. But the breaking point occurred when the youth group sponsored the appearance of the radical black activist Stokely Carmichael. Richard describes that event that took place, like the dances, in St. Margaret's basement:

> *Stokely was very late, and I began to think he wouldn't come. When he and his entourage arrived there were at least three men leading the way. They immediately told the audience that they would have to be seated before Stokely would come in. When he did enter the room, he had bodyguards on both sides and behind him. I don't know if they were armed, but they didn't smile, and like the Secret Service, they watched the crowd continuously. I can't remember one thing verbatim that Stokely said to us, but I do recollect that his speech was very militant and threatening. I was worried that someone might provoke a shouting match. I was relieved the visit was short, that they quickly departed.*

At the end of Bill's one-year curacy, he was called to a church in Roxbury, Massachusetts. When the vestry asked Richard and me to step down as youth sponsors, we left St. Margaret's and joined our friends Ron and Mary Ellen Durbin in the Roman Catholic underground community Vatican II and a Half, where our radical actions (compared to such spectacular deeds on a national scale as the draft file burnings by the Berrigan brothers) seemed barely left of center. Anglicans though we were, we were welcomed. Vatican II and a Half met on Sundays in the gymnasium of the school connected to St. Philip Neri Church. Jeff Danzig, the young assistant priest who led the group, had studied in the Netherlands with Father Edward Schillebeeckx, the liberal theologian who wrote the popular and progressive New Dutch Catechism, which would never receive the imprimatur of approval by the Roman Catholic Church. (Although not officially condemned, Father Schillebeeckx would be summoned to the Vatican to be questioned three times in the 1980s. He would continue to write until his death at the age of ninety-five in 2009.)

The hundred or so people who attended the Vatican II and a Half Mass on Sunday mornings were deeply committed to social change: they registered people to vote; they worked on housing for the homeless; they volunteered in soup kitchens. The Mass was informal, but that was fine with us. We felt comfortable in offbeat churches. (At the San Juan Navajo Episcopal Mission that we'd attended in Farmington, New Mexico, it was common for dogs—and once, a gobbling turkey—to stroll up and down the aisle during services.)

The sermons were group discussions—often about an aspect of Roman Catholic theology. People did not hesitate to say how their lives were affected by pronouncements from the Vatican. But while the discussions were interesting, Richard and I didn't attend that group because we were interested in dogma; we were there because we loved the community, which took seriously the twenty-fifth chapter of St. Matthew's Gospel with its injunction to feed the hungry, clothe the naked and welcome the stranger.

South Shore had once been a Jewish neighborhood, but its population was now half African American. In recognition of the change, a venerable old delicatessen on Sixty-ninth Street had placed a sign in its window advertising "kosher soul food."

Right after midnight one Fourth of July, the woman in the basement apartment beneath us gave birth to her baby in the toilet, and after her sister banged on our door, Richard and I threw on our bathrobes and ran downstairs. "Do something!" Richard yelled at me. Terrified, I fished the baby out of the toilet and wrapped him in the bottom part of my white terrycloth robe. I wiped the baby's nose and mouth and tapped his feet until he breathed, but I had no idea what to do about the umbilical cord that dangled between the mother's legs as she tottered to her bed, pulling the baby and me, like Siamese twins, after her.

Two young policemen, one black and one white, arrived. The white policeman lit a cigarette and peered down into the mother's crotch. "I'm in charge here," he said, and he ordered me out of the room. I was kneeling by the mother's bed—she had not yet delivered the afterbirth; the cord, of course, had not been cut; the baby was wrapped in my robe and I was still wearing it. What in the world did that cop expect me to do?

When I told the policeman I would hold the baby until the home delivery team from Cook County Hospital arrived, he threatened to arrest me. What I said next I don't remember—something disrespectful, of course—but my retort made the black policeman laugh. This infuriated his partner, who stalked over to Richard and told him he was taking me in for "interfering with the duties of a police officer."

Would I be the first of my friends to be thrown in jail? Wow! Fortunately, before I could make any more sarcastic comments, Richard stepped in. In addition to his federal job, he was in an urban studies graduate program at Loyola University. He had the presence of mind to mention the name of one of his professors who was chairman of the Chicago Police Review Board, and the policeman, showing better judgment than I, withdrew his complaint. Had I actually been put into a crowded Chicago jail cell, I would have been scared out of my mind. The maternity delivery team arrived from Cook County Hospital, the police left and Richard and I went back upstairs to bed.

Chicago in the 1960s was where things happened, but as Patrick reminded us, the sky was gray. As soon as we returned from our Phoenix vacation, Richard began looking for a government transfer. The following summer, we loaded Patrick; our three-year-old son, Christopher; and our six-month-old baby girl, Noelle, into our red Volkswagen bus and began a leisurely, circuitous trek toward the San Carlos Apache Reservation in eastern Arizona. We meandered through the South, stopping first in Kentucky, at Berea College, to visit an old friend of my mother's, Minnie Maude Macauley. As our van pulled up in front of the Boone Tavern Hotel, two smiling college boys with short hair handed us copies of the radical underground newspaper the *Great Speckled Bird.*

"You Yankees think the action's up North," one of them said politely, "but the Southland's where it's really happening."

After attending a service at an Appalachian mountain church and visiting Richard's relatives in Charleston, West Virginia, we drove back through the hills of Kentucky and Tennessee and on to Dallas to see Christopher's godmother, Johanna Clevenger, and her husband, Geral Dietz, friends from the Navajo Reservation, who were doing residencies at Parkland Hospital. As we stood in the cramped space of Trauma Room One where John Kennedy once lay, I recalled November 22, 1963, when Richard rushed to Chandler High School, where I was teaching a class in American literature, to tell me of the president's assassination. Later that afternoon, my doctor told me I was pregnant with our first child. He would be named Patrick, after the dead president's dead baby boy.

Leaving Dallas, we drove through the night and reached Gallup, New Mexico, with the dawn. Giddy with both lack of sleep and the excitement of being back in the Southwest, we could not contain our hilarity as we trooped into the Ranch Kitchen out on Route 66 west of town. We knew we were home when, at the table next to us, a large Navajo family in traditional dress nodded to us with friendly smiles. Before we had gone to Chicago, we had lived for a year and a half on the Navajo Reservation at Shiprock, New Mexico, ninety miles north of Gallup. Although we had never been to San Carlos, we knew the Western Apaches were related to the Navajos. We would not be going into alien territory. Would we?

SIX YEARS EARLIER, I had taken my month-old baby, boarded an old Frontier airplane in Phoenix and headed off for the Navajo Reservation where Richard had already moved our belongings and signed on with the Bureau of Indian Affairs. His work as a vocational training and employment counselor was hardly what he had envisioned back in the psychology department at Arizona State University, but when I became pregnant and was asked to resign from my teaching job, Richard withdrew from graduate school, took the Federal Services Entrance Examination and accepted the first position offered to him.

"Two years with Indian Affairs, that's all," Richard said. Perhaps we could do this instead of the Peace Corps, something we'd once, sort of halfheartedly, thought about. Two years. I hoped Richard was right. If I had known that I would be moving not merely to another state but to another world, and not for two years but for twelve, would I have boarded that airplane?

When Richard met Patrick and me at the little airport in Farmington, New Mexico, he seemed distracted. He did not talk much as he settled luggage, diaper bag, Patrick and me into our 1957 Dodge. I noticed a broom in the back seat. How odd, I thought, as we drove out of the parking lot and headed west toward Shiprock. As I started to ask about the broom, I glanced over at Richard and saw on his face a look of pure despair.

"What's wrong?" I asked. "Tell me."

"It's our government quarters," Richard said. "They're kind of...primitive."

"Primitive?"

"And there are wild dogs. One of them bit me. Right through my boot."

"*What?*"

"Dr. Dietz at the Indian Health Hospital told me to call him if the dog foamed at the mouth." I stared at Richard. "Dietz said to have you call him if I died." He tried to laugh. "Don't worry," he said. "The dog's not rabid."

When we pulled up across from what Richard told me was the Shiprock Boarding School, I looked around me, dazed. On one side of the street, stark wooden dormitories with peeling paint rose up, in bleak isolation, from a field of prairie grass. The place looked like a prison.

"We live over here," Richard said, indicating a cinder block duplex across from the school. In front of the duplex several mongrel dogs rolled around in the dirt, growling and biting each other. They perked up their ears and lunged toward us when Richard turned off the engine. I watched in horror as the dogs circled the car, jumping and yelping. Suddenly, a geyser erupted from somewhere in the dirt and, strong and steady as a fireman's hose, spewed muddy water directly on the front door.

"The lawn sprinkler," Richard said.

"But there's no *lawn*!"

"There's not much water, either. It's mostly silt from the bottom of the San Juan River."

"How long does it stay on?" I asked.

"Half an hour. Twice a day."

I looked down at my new baby in his soft little nightgown with the tiny yellow flowers and the drawstring at the bottom. And then I watched in silence as the sprinkler pelted the door of the duplex with a steady and powerful stream of mud. When the sprinkler turned off, Richard reached in the back of the car for the broom.

"Stay in the car until I tell you to get out and then run like hell," he said. He swung the broomstick at the dogs as I ran, clutching the baby, to the door, which opened directly into the kitchen. The first thing I saw when I entered my new home was the wooden door attached to metal legs we'd used as a desk our last year at Arizona State. Across the top of the door Richard had arranged cinder blocks into shelves that were piled high with our wedding dishes, pots and pans and a few groceries.

"There aren't any cupboards," Richard said, "so I improvised."

"It looks like a basement boiler room," I said as I looked around at the maze of pipes that ran up the walls and across the ceilings. There were no shades at the windows. I awoke the next morning to see a bunch of Navajo children giggling at me through the glass. Richard laughed and waved at them while I covered my head with a pillow and cried.

On the Wednesday evening of my first week in Shiprock, we loaded the reeking, overflowing twenty-gallon diaper pail into the Dodge and drove the thirty miles back to Farmington. By the time we had spent nearly two hours at the laundromat and found our way to the Piggly Wiggly supermarket, it was 7:30 p.m. When we discovered the Piggly Wiggly closed at 8:00, we each grabbed a shopping cart and half of our two-week grocery list and began rushing up and down aisles. Patrick lay in the baby carrier across the top of my cart. Whenever he cried I popped a bottle into his mouth. As the manager announced over the loudspeaker that the store was closed, Richard caught up with me. He was pushing a cart full of bread.

"Is that all you've got?" I asked him. "Just bread? What about all the other stuff on the list?" He stared down at the display of day-old bread he'd grabbed by mistake and then turned and raced back to the bakery section to retrieve his cart.

"I found everything but the chopped olives," I told him when he returned. I popped another bottle into Patrick's mouth as the manager announced for the second time that the store was closed. Richard sprinted ahead of me to the checkout counter and spoke to the clerk.

"Hey, Joe!" blared the clerk over the loudspeaker. "We got any chopped olives in the back?"

"How many you want?" boomed Joe. "A case?"

"You want a case?" Richard asked me as I parked my cart behind him.

"A six-ounce can," I whispered.

"A six-ounce can, Joe!" bellowed the clerk.

As the clerk rang up the last of the groceries, I lifted Patrick in his baby carrier to the conveyer belt. His blue eyes stared up at me like marbles.

"Bingo!" the clerk said as he pushed a button. "Today's double Green Stamp day!" I watched as rolls and rolls of Green Stamps spewed across Patrick's stomach.

"We made it," I said to Richard. I took a deep breath and relaxed.

"Uh oh," the clerk said. "Poor little baby got sick."

I whipped around to see Patrick, Green Stamps and conveyer belt covered with curdled milk. Later, in the back seat of the Dodge, I stripped the baby of his wet, sour clothes and struggled to change his dirty diaper while Richard swerved around traffic to get back to a Mexican restaurant that closed at 9:00. I began to laugh. I hiccupped, gulped and giggled as tears of hysteria poured down my face. That day became the prototype for all of our Saturdays: laundromat, supermarket, Mexican restaurant. We soon added the liquor store to the itinerary when we discovered that a jug of California sherry fortified us through the rest of the week.

The children who had peeked in our bedroom window on my first morning visited us often that summer. They always asked to see the baby. I loved, especially, a four-year-old named Pinto, who did, indeed, look like a little round bean. One day in late August, Pinto did not come with the other children, and when I asked where he was, they looked wide eyed at each other and then one of them looked at me and said, shyly, "Pinto drowned in the river."

I stared at the children, stunned; they quickly went away, and I never saw them again. I did not know then that Navajos avoid speaking of the dead. My question surely upset them as much as their answer did me. I have a picture Richard took one evening of the seven children clustered around Patrick and me. Two little boys sit on each side of us on the sofa, and another boy and two girls kneel in a line on the floor in front. The boys and one of the girls wear jeans and T-shirts, and the other girl wears a print dress. The

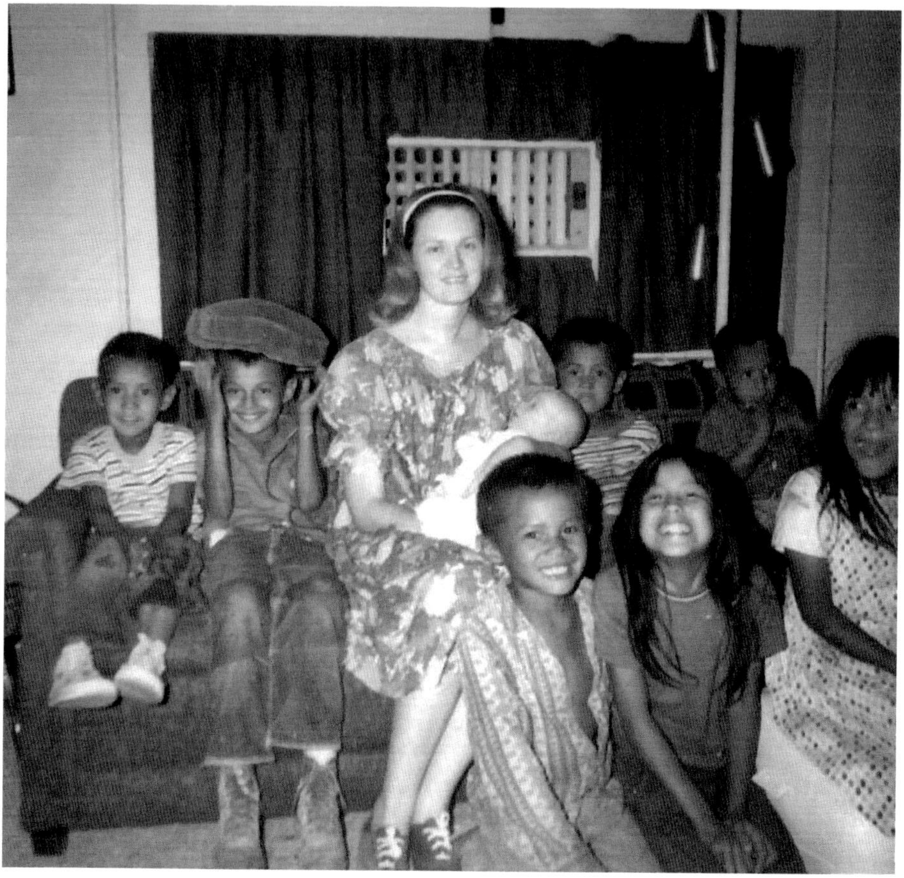

I am holding my baby boy, Patrick, and we are surrounded by the Navajo children who visited us often in Shiprock, New Mexico.

children are clowning and posing (one boy next to me holds a round pillow on top of his head) and they are laughing—all except one little boy who sucks his fingers and looks away from the camera.

After a year in that mud-splattered house with the wild dogs, we received permission from the BIA superintendent to move across from the hospital into a wonderful house made of rock and wood where the whole south wall was a cooling, vine-draped window that looked out at the great Shiprock itself—that volcanic explosion that slopes like the Great Wall of China down the high desert.

The Four Corners is the exact spot where the states of Arizona, New Mexico, Colorado and Utah fit together in a perfect cross. Richard's job

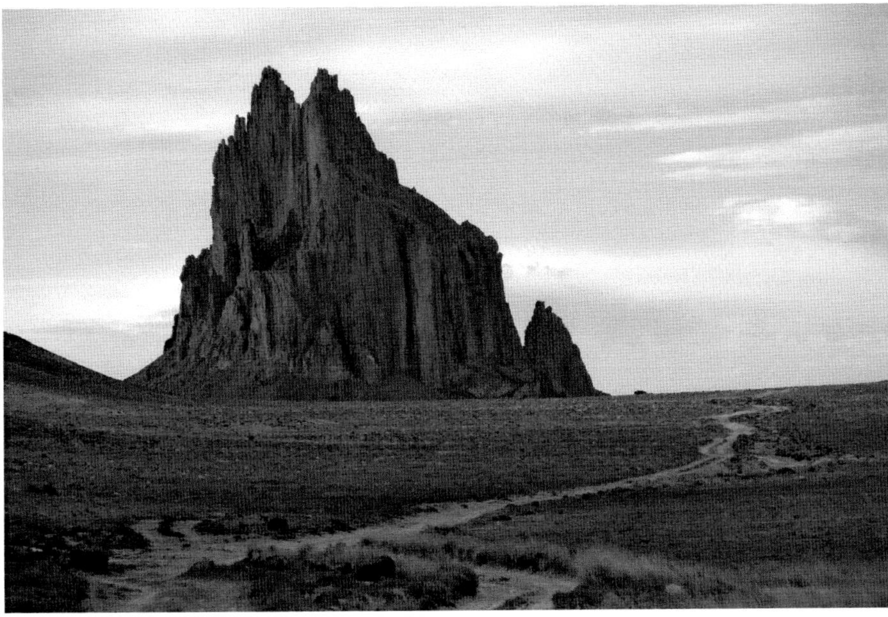

From the living room of our government quarters we could see the Shiprock, the sacred mountain of the Navajo people.

was to drive the Four Corners looking for people in remote places that were nearly impossible to find. After he got lost for ten hours one night, the BIA assigned him a Navajo guide and interpreter by the name of Willy Bruce. Willy Bruce woke us up one midnight by banging on our door. He wanted to take us to a Sing, a healing ceremony, he said, and he told us to hurry up and get the baby and get going. I tried to keep my eyes from closing as Willy drove us in his pickup to the fairgrounds, where we joined a huge crowd of Navajos. There was a bonfire, but except for that light, it was dark and silent. I saw a lone woman who sat on a pile of Navajo rugs. She wore a velvet blouse and a long skirt, her hair was twisted with twine into a bun and turquoise hung from her ears and covered her arms. The woman did not move at all: she did not fidget or scratch or twitch or blink her eyelids; she seemed almost not to breathe. We watched as the *hataalii*, the medicine man, sang the woman back into harmony. Even though we were the only *bilagaana*, the only white people, at that Night Chant, no one seemed to mind or even to notice. Once I got over being self-conscious, I found myself being carried along by the *hataalii*'s haunting, repetitive chant, and for the first time since I was a child, I had a tantalizing, fleeting glimpse of a blending of physical and spiritual worlds.

In the fall, we went down to Window Rock for the Navajo Tribal Fair. The day was perfect Arizona autumn: sixty-five degrees, and the sun shone gold and mellow. I was carrying Patrick in my arms, and as I walked next to Richard through the crowd, for the first and only time in my life, I fainted. When I woke up Richard was carrying me. I looked up at the sky to see Patrick's head bobbing above me. He was riding on the shoulders of a hefty Navajo man who was laughing at the comments people were shouting at him. Later, as I lay, chilled with flu, on a bed in the house of a BIA employee and his wife, I asked what all of those people had been shouting about. My hostess laughed. "They were teasing the man. They wanted to know where a Navajo got a blond, blue-eyed baby."

The Navajo teenage girls at San Juan Episcopal Mission called Patrick *Na dotl'izhi*, which they told me meant "blue eyes." I practiced saying *Na dotl'izhi* with the glottal stop way back in my throat until the girls told me I sounded exactly right.

The Navajo language is very close to some Apache dialects, which is not surprising because the Navajo people are a subgroup of the Western Apache. I had heard Navajos say they understood Apache almost as if it were their own language. Years later, I would be told by Apaches at San Carlos that when they hear Navajo spoken they think they should be able to understand but they cannot; what sounds so familiar seems just beyond their grasp. This became clear to me when I would say *Na dotl'izhi* and the Apaches would laugh. They would tell me that what I said was not "blue eyes" at all. They would tell me that what I said was "skunk."

San Carlos

On the morning of July 5, 1970, our VW bus chugged along U.S. Route 70, east of the old silver mining town of Globe and west of the pioneer Mormon community of Safford. Several miles back we had passed a large wooden sign in the shape of an arrow announcing the western boundary of the San Carlos Apache Reservation. Ocotillo plants, yuccas and mesquite trees looked nearly transparent in the glare of the sun. To our right the desert floor curved upward into a flat-topped hill that resembled a bucket turned upside down. To the northeast rose a mountain of three peaks called the Triplets.

Outside, the temperature was 113 degrees Fahrenheit. Inside our VW bus, even with all the windows opened wide and wind roaring through, it was more like 125. The sudden apprehension I had felt upon crossing the reservation border turned to contentment. Although I had never before been to this particular place, it was familiar: it was desert, it was heat, it was Arizona and I was home.

"Are we almost there, Dad?" Patrick asked.

"Almost," Richard said.

"That's what you said hours ago."

"Well, this time it's true," Richard promised.

"I'm thirsty," whined Christopher. His tongue hung out of his round face, and he panted dramatically. I went back to the second seat and pushed the spigot lever on the big green Coleman jug to fill the boys' plastic cups with water. "Yuck!" Chris yelled. "Noelle's throwing up!" I looked down at the

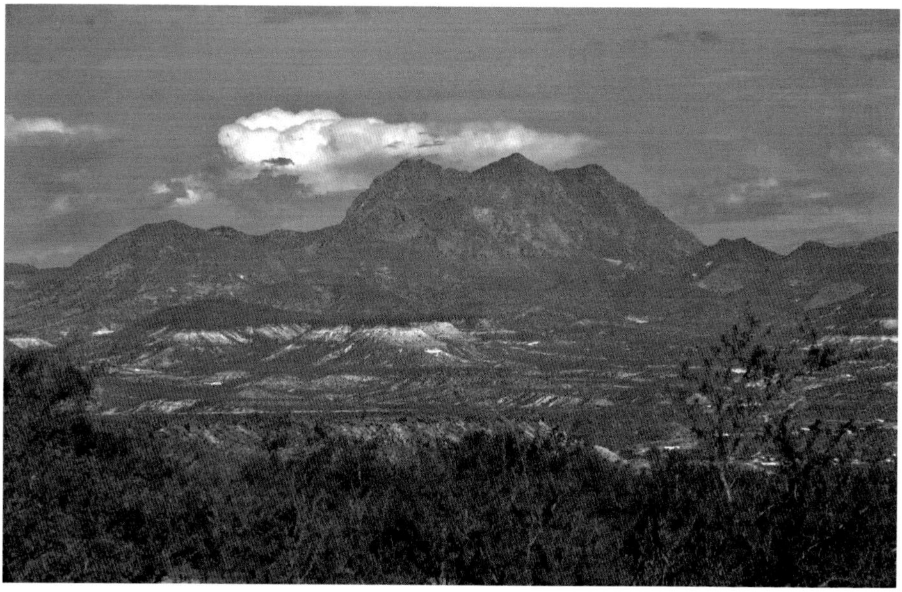

The Triplets Mountain rises above the town of San Carlos.

white wicker bassinette on the floor of the bus where the baby hummed to her hands as they darted back and forth like butterflies. Curdled milk dribbled down her chin and formed a pool at the base of her neck. In the middle of the pool floated a dead bee. "Yuck!" Chris shouted again as I grabbed a handful of Kleenex and dabbed at the bee and sour milk.

"She ate it!" Patrick said.

"Ate what?" Richard asked.

"That makes me sick," Pat said. "She ate it and then threw up!"

"Ate what?" Richard asked again.

"A bee," I told him.

"Maybe it stung her insides!" Chris said. He stared at his sister, fascinated. She smiled and reached a sticky hand to his hair. He jerked back and wrinkled his nose. "The bee was probably dead to begin with," I said, hoping I was right. I finished cleaning the baby's chin and neck and took her back with me to the front seat.

"Hey, Chris, look!" Patrick said, when we turned north off the highway and onto a road paved in melting asphalt. "There's a real Indian up there on that rock!"

The Apache stood on the bluff high above us. He wore a red headband, and his hair fell to his shoulders. He watched as we followed the road around the bluff and then we lost sight of him. We drove down into a small oasis of cottonwood trees whose roots appeared to have sunk deep and sucked up any available water from the dry San Carlos River bed. The leaves of those tall, old trees were as green as the peridot that was mined on the reservation, giving off an aura of coolness in that dry, brown landscape.

Appropriately, the first place we passed was the Peridot Trading Company, a white stone building with two gasoline pumps and a Union sign. We wound around another bluff, crossed a bridge over a dry wash, bumped over the ridges of a cattle guard and came upon, in the middle of the desert, a main street four blocks long. Behind juniper, palm and eucalyptus trees stood solid old houses constructed of large squares of yellow-brown tufa stone. Pampas grass swayed gently around the windows. Across the front of each house, held up by chunky stone pillars, ran a wide covered porch from which hung an old-fashioned glider swing. The houses looked solid, rooted, as if they had been there forever. They did not resemble any government quarters I had ever seen.

"Is this where we're gonna live?" Patrick asked as Richard pulled into the parking lot at the Bureau of Indian Affairs. "Way out here in the middle of nowhere?"

We all got out of the bus and looked around. Next to the government building, which also housed the tribal offices, was the tribe general store. On the front porch of the tribe store stood a line of older Apache men and one old woman. They stared at us.

"Those people are watching us," Patrick said.

"Everybody's black but us," Christopher said. "Just like Chicago."

"They're not black," Patrick said. "They're Indians."

"Hey, Dave!" someone called. "Richard David!" A short, stocky man strolled toward us, puffing on a pipe. He removed the pipe from his mouth and shook hands with Richard. "Almost didn't recognize you with that beard, Dave," the man said. I was struck by his slow, deliberate way of speaking and his deep, growly voice. "I saw your red bus, there, with those flower stickers plastered on it, and those Illinois license plates, and I said to myself, here come some more Chicago hippies out to live like the Indians!" He chuckled. "See, Dave," he repeated, "I almost didn't recognize you."

I recognized him. Over the years, Richard had described the BIA superintendent, Ted Whitebull, perfectly. Other than the fact that his face with its high cheekbones and aquiline nose could have been sculpted on a Dakota mountain, this Oneida-Sioux Indian would not have looked out of place on Michigan Avenue in Chicago. He wore a starched white shirt with a tie and a navy blazer with brass buttons that glittered painfully in the white-hot sun. It seemed to me that Ted Whitebull's surface reflected the paradox of his character: he was happily married to a white woman; he was a social worker with a bootstrap philosophy; and he was probably the only registered Republican with a grandfather who had died at Wounded Knee.

"How long's it been since we've seen each other, Ted?" Richard asked. "Five or six years?"

"Six." Ted puffed on his pipe. "You'd barely arrived in Shiprock, New Mexico, see, when I came out from Chicago for that meeting. Remember? Hmmm?" He puffed some more. "You were right out of college. Out to save the world. You and Lyndon Johnson." He laughed. "You Democrats." He smiled at me. "Now, introduce me to your family, Dave."

"Hello, Mr. Whitebull," I said, as I shifted Noelle from one arm to the other and disentangled her fingers from one of my hoop earrings. My wrinkled mini-skirt seemed to be crawling up my thighs.

"Ted," he said.

"Ted," I repeated, painfully conscious of my hot, sweaty palm and his cool, dry one as we shook hands. Didn't the man even perspire?

"I'm glad you folks decided to come to San Carlos," Ted said. "Use some of that community organizing stuff you learned in Chicago, Dave. I hope you'll like it here."

I hoped so, too, but would the feeling be mutual? Would they like us? The line of Apaches in front of the tribe store had not moved. They continued to watch us as we pulled out of the parking lot and drove off in search of our quarters.

"Everywhere [were] the...suspicious faces of the...Indians challenging you," I'd read in an old memoir about this very place. "You felt the challenge in your very marrow—that unspoken challenge to prove yourself anything else than one more liar and thief, differing but little from the procession of liars and thieves who preceded you." Britton Davis, the young but surprisingly sympathetic lieutenant fresh out of West Point, wrote that about the San Carlos Apaches of 1882.* Eighty-eight years later, I knew exactly what Lieutenant Davis meant.

Both the tribe and town of San Carlos take their name from the San Carlos River, which, according to the historian Elliott Coues, was apparently named after the king of Spain, Carlos III, by the Spanish Franciscan priest

---

*. Britton Davis, *The Truth About Geronimo* (New Haven, CT: Yale University Press, 1929, 1963).

and explorer Francisco Garces. On November 28, 1775, Garces refers in his diary to the Rio de Carlos. Coincidentally, November 4 had been the feast of St. Charles Borromeo, a Counter Reformation priest who died in 1584, which made it possible to add "San" to the name of the river.*

For the first few months in San Carlos, although I felt unsettled and unsure of how I would fit in, I was certainly not isolated. My next-door neighbor, Irene, who was married to the BIA roads engineer, Frank Peres, gave a coffee to introduce me to the other BIA wives. Joan, the wife of Arnie Gass, one of the new doctors at the Indian Health Service, invited Christopher to play with her son, J.J. Sister Anne Regina, Patrick's first-grade teacher at the Catholic mission school, was kind and welcoming.

Although we did not live in a government compound such as the one where the Indian Health Service employees lived, our house was a rectangular, government-issue stucco box identical to theirs. The beautiful stone houses on the main street, we learned, were inhabited by BIA employees who had lived at San Carlos for years. We shared a street with such diverse neighbors as the tribal chairman's son, who lived in a trailer across from us, and the Blessed Sacrament Sisters in their convent behind the mission.

Even though I had longed to be in the Southwest, I dearly missed the urban community we had left behind. Chicago had been so intense that I had felt perpetually wired for action; now I was finding it impossible to gear down. Nevertheless, in spite of feeling that I did not yet belong to this new place, I rejoiced, after four frigid midwestern winters, in the glorious climate. That first fall, winter and spring, we often took the children out to San Carlos Lake. They loved to walk up to the dam to see the two stone eagles that decorated the spillway side, a reminder of the days when real eagles nested in the small mountain that formed the dam's eastern edge. Spring of 1971 was vintage Arizona, and we would stand on the bridge and look over the water at the dusty blues, pinks and lavenders of the distant desert. Leaning lazily against the concrete wall, I would try to focus on a mountain, shimmering, iridescent, one hundred miles to the north. Focusing was a problem for me since coming home to Arizona; my myopia seemed worse than it had been in Chicago, where everything was so close together. Were my eyes getting weaker? Or had I lost the habit of seeing? Paradoxically, looking out into that pastel haze calmed and centered me, helped me to focus inwardly, at least, and gradually, I felt the intensity of the last few years drain away.

As we drove through the Sonoran Desert between San Carlos and Tucson or Phoenix, I looked with awe on the things I had taken for granted as a

*. Elliott Coues, *Arizona Place Names* (Tucson: University of Arizona Press, 1988), 381.

child: the spiny, green-barked paloverde trees; the ocotillos, waving their red-tipped "monkey tails" like ocean ferns in the wind; and the saguaro cacti, the gods of the desert, their great arms raised to the sky. I savored the warmth of the sun upon my skin, inhaled the sudden bursts of mesquite borne upon the quiet desert breezes, cherished the rare display of wildflowers coaxed awake by the perfect blend of fall rains and spring temperatures: the desert marigold; the fragile fairy duster; the lavender verbena; the orange globemallow; the beautiful chuparosa with its many red blossoms; and my favorite, the lovely soft pink Mexican Evening Primrose. I realized I had not merely missed the desert, I had been starved for it. I was ravenous, and I tried to devour it. I wanted to embrace the earth, the plants, the air, the sun. I could not get enough, and for the first time I understood why people returning from exile would kneel down and kiss dirt.

"ALL I KNOW," MY neighbor Irene told me that day when we picked ripe chili peppers in the field near Safford to make *ristras* to hang on our porches, "is that after we handled those medicine sticks and headdresses we found in the

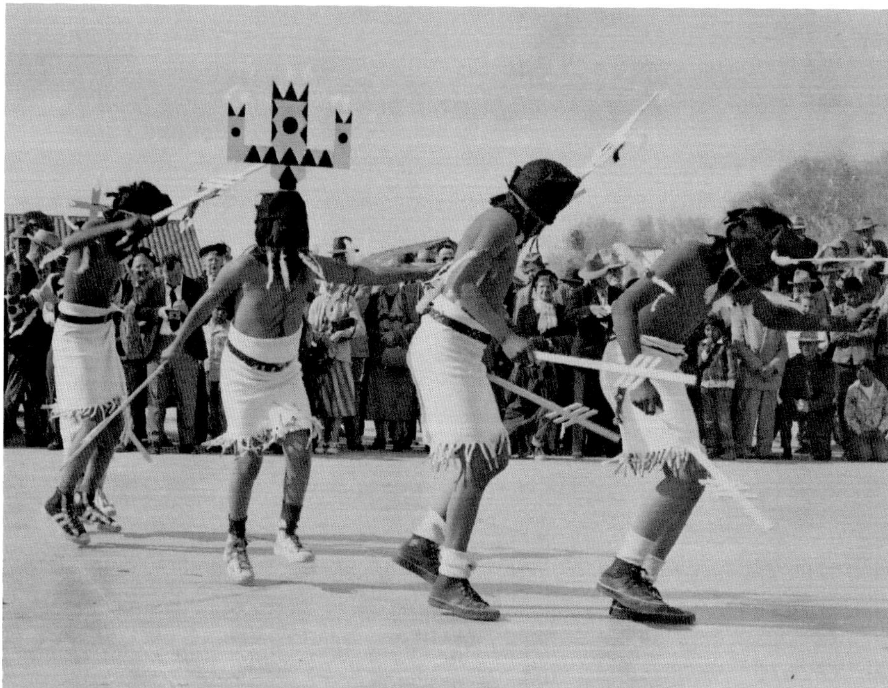

Gáán dancers perform in a parade. *Photo by Russell J. Mishler.*

cave, we all got sick. I didn't get as sick as the other folks because I didn't take any of that stuff home. They did. For souvenirs. And they threw up all night. Had chills and fever. The works. I got off a lot easier, only a little nauseated from the heat, because I refused to bring that stuff into my house."

"What kind of headdresses?" I asked, starting to feel slightly nauseated myself. The back of my shoulders hurt from stooping to pull the bright red chilies from their bushes and stuffing them into my bag. My nose began to run, and my eyes burned from the combination of capsicum and dust.

"You know, those flat, painted wooden things the devil dancers wear," Irene said.

I'd been in San Carlos long enough to know that "devil dancer" was not an Apache term. Irene was referring to Gáán dancers, the Apache men who put on masks to become spirits from the mountain. It was evangelical Christian missionaries who saw evil in native religion and called the Gáán dancers devils. Over the next five years, I would attend ceremonials where representatives from many tribes would dance. Much of the performing would seem similar, but when the Apaches in their black hoods and tall wooden crowns would take the floor with their distinctive drum cadence, an extraordinary silence always fell over the audience.

MY FIRST TWO INDIAN visitors did not wear masks and crowns. They wore yellow hard hats and carried tool chests. They came to repair a window in my kitchen.

"Your kid break a window?" the good-looking one asked. He looked me up and down and then winked.

"Heh heh," laughed the other one, who made me think, instantly, of Barney Rubble. He was short and round, and chunks of black hair poked out around his face from beneath his hard hat.

"My name's Raleigh," the first man said, "and this here's my buddy Ralph."

"Hi," I said. "I'm Sonja."

"We already know that," Raleigh said. "How do you like living out here with us wild Apaches, Sonja?" He winked at me, again. "You better watch out, we might scalp you! Right Ralph?"

"Heh heh!" laughed Ralph, again, who, I discovered, was not an Apache but a Pima, from Sacaton, on the Gila River Indian reservation near our hometown of Chandler. Raleigh and Ralph arrived from the plant management office whenever anything went wrong in our government quarters. While they peered into the oven, turned spigots or handed wrenches back and forth, Raleigh talked, and Ralph and I laughed.

The Goode girls lived in a trailer down the street. The girls (who pronounced their last name "Goody") often came to our house to play. Rosie was five, Christopher's age, and Mariam, Rosie's aunt, was twelve. Mariam was a child with special needs. "I love you, Sonja; I love you, Nellie," she would call out whenever she saw us. The girls carried Noelle around the living room trying to make her walk. "Walk, Nellie," they commanded, balancing Noelle between the two of them. "Walk, Nellie." They did this until Noelle was nine months old and took her first steps. The girls arrived early one autumn evening when Noelle and I were in the front yard.

"Nellie, I love you!" Mariam cried, as she picked up Noelle and twirled her around. Noelle's thatch of yellow hair and her pink cotton dress billowed out in the breeze. "Moom?" she cried, pointing to the sky. "Moom?" Rosie got there before I could. "That's right, Nellie," Rosie said as she carefully took Noelle from Mariam's arms. "Moon."

"I want to carry Nellie!" Mariam's lips quivered.

"Why don't we let Nellie walk by herself?" I said. "Remember how you helped her learn?"

"OK," Mariam said as Rosie gently lowered Noelle to the ground.

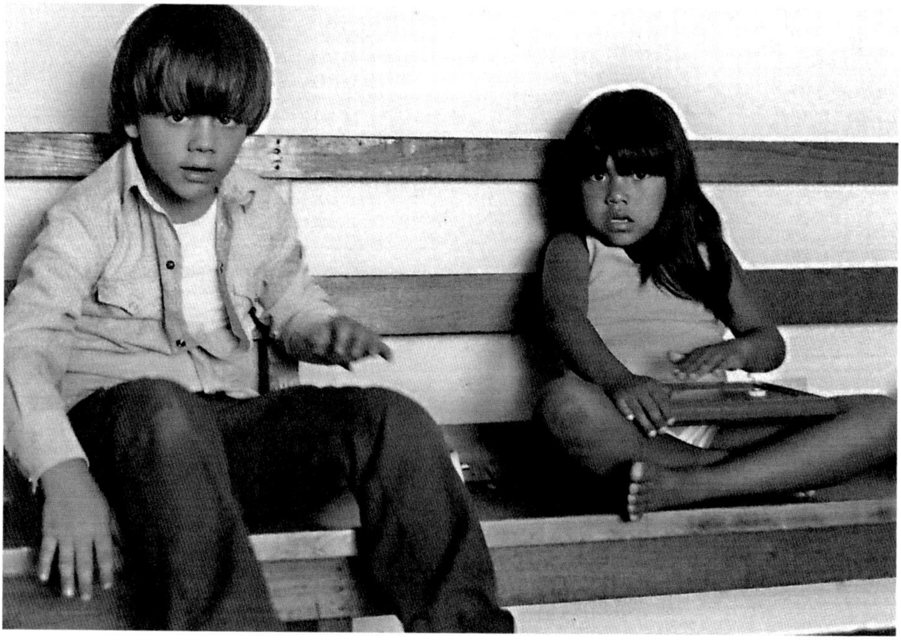

Our son Christopher and his good friend Rosie collected old pottery shards from a construction site in San Carlos.

Christopher and Rosie found pottery shards on a construction site near the school. They brought them to our house in a paper sack and dumped them on the living room floor. They worked for hours trying to fit pieces of the black zigzags together, and I was amazed when they came up with a match.

ONE DAY, PATRICK NOTICED a girl. "Mom, you should see her," he told me. "She has long black hair, and it goes all the way down her back. It's kind of curly. Her name's Maria." He pointed Maria out to me one Sunday when we sat behind her family in church: father, mother and three little girls. They were not just good-looking—they were gorgeous, every one of them, with their olive skin, black hair and dark eyes. Patrick's crush reminded me of my own first love who, like Maria, was Hispanic.

"What was Maria wearing today?" Richard asked Patrick as we walked home from church.

"A pink dress with white dots," Patrick said. "And white hair ribbons."

On Valentine's Day, Patrick went to school carrying his valentines in a brown paper bag. In that bag there was a special valentine not cut from the book like all the others. This valentine was handmade—*heartmade*—for

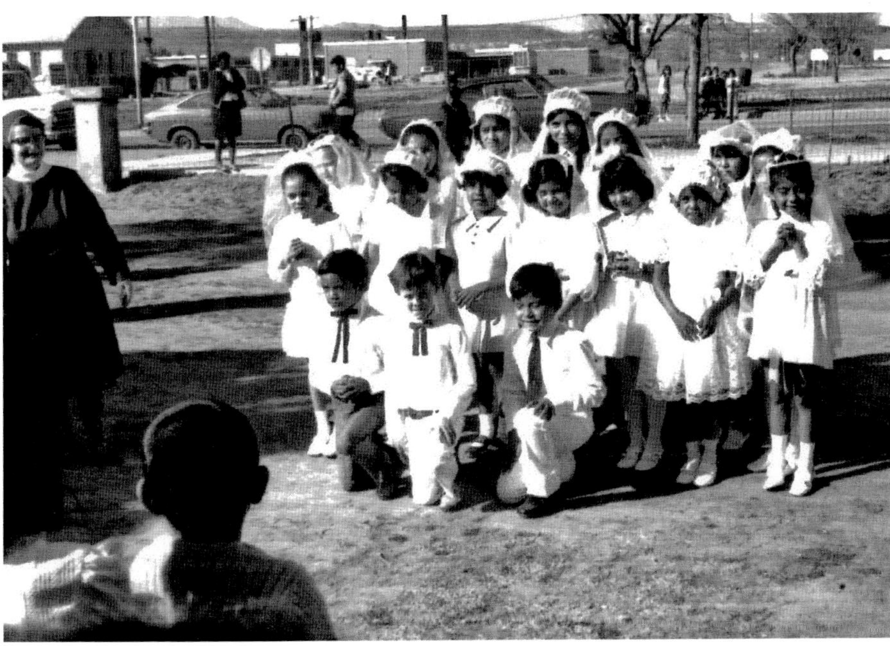

In this photograph of Patrick's First Communion class, he is kneeling in the middle of the front row.

a girl whose hair curled all the way down her back. When Patrick came home from school that afternoon, he threw the paper bag on the table and I looked inside. Three valentines? What about the other nineteen kids in class? Didn't the teacher make sure the kids gave valentines to everyone? This was a Catholic school for heaven's sake! What was wrong with these nuns?

"Look, Pat," I said, my heart aching for him. "It's because you're new and you don't know many kids yet."

Patrick stared at the floor. "What about Maria? Did she like her valentine?" He scrunched his eyebrows together. "Patrick?"

"She held it up in front of the whole class and made fun of me. Everyone laughed."

"Oh, Patrick," I said, reaching out to hug him. "It's because you're new," I called after him as he stomped down the hall and slammed his bedroom door.

At a potluck after church one Sunday, Richard and I stood with the children in a long line of people that wound around the edges of the parish hall. An old woman wearing battered tennis shoes trudged heavily up to us, her pink Apache camp dress dragging the floor. Her voluminous over blouse was held together by safety pins. Strands of gray hair fell down from the bun at the back of her head.

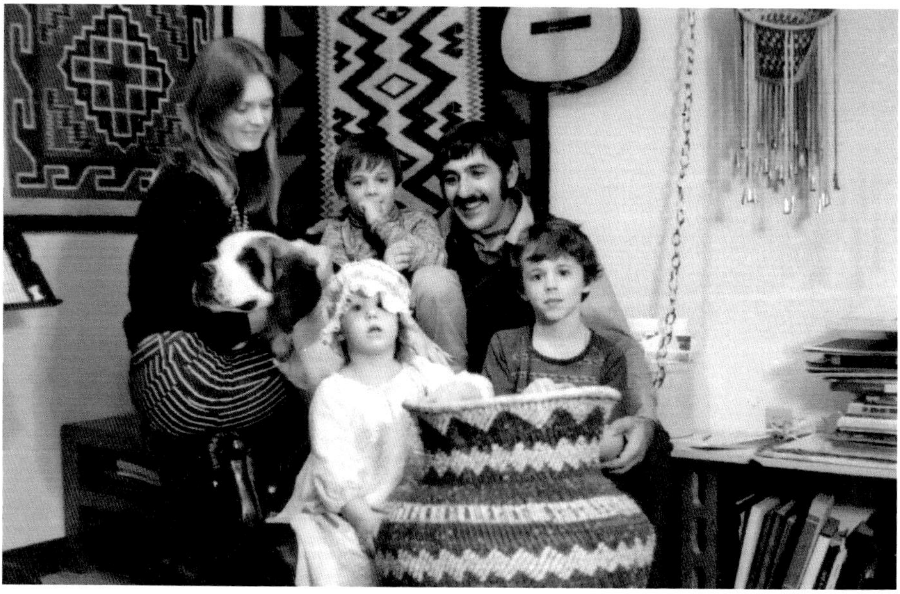

For our second Christmas card from San Carlos, we posed with our Apache olla basket.

"I am Martha," she said, giving us a gap-toothed smile of extraordinary sweetness. "Did you know my son, Anthony Machukay, at the American Indian Center in Chicago?"

"Oh, yes, of course!" Richard said. "The first time I met him he was playing the piano. Jazz. He was good!"

Martha nodded and smiled. "My son is coming home. Did you know he got a job with the Arizona Indian Commission?"

"No, I didn't, Martha," Richard said, "but that's wonderful. I'm glad to hear it."

"Anthony, he says he's tired of Chicago."

"Me, too," Richard agreed.

Martha laughed. "You, too?" she asked, pointing her lip at me. "You happy to be here?"

"Well, I guess so…" I thought of my own son. Martha touched my hand. "It's good, you come back to Arizona," she said. "It's good you come home."

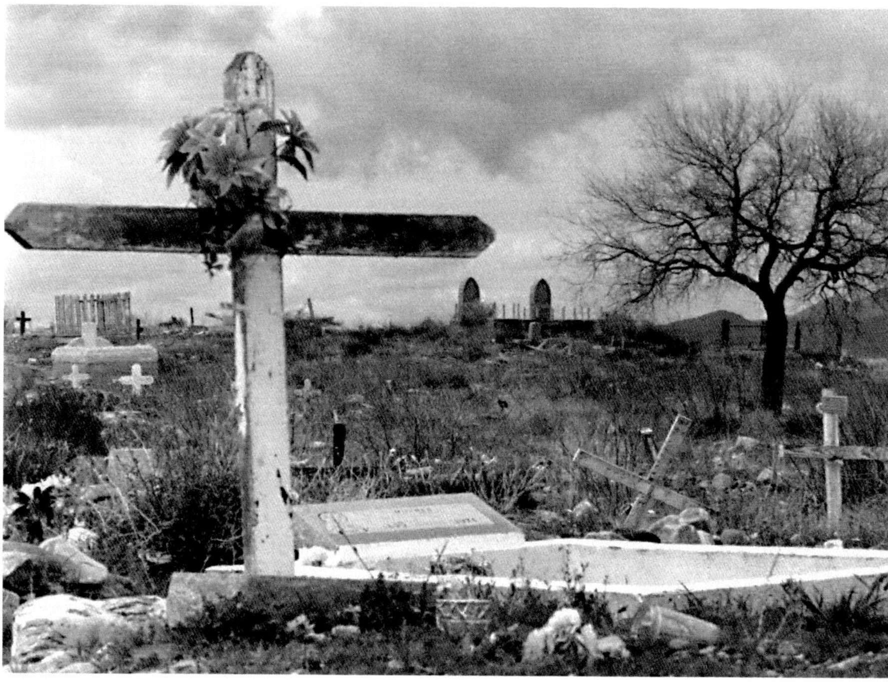

San Carlos Cemetery, 1971.

Funeral

The following summer, I cursed the heat, but this time I sat, not in a sweltering VW bus, but on the edge of a folding chair in the midst of several hundred mourners on a basketball court in a big blue aluminum building called Burdette Hall. I squirmed with discomfort as I strained for a glimpse of the closed coffin that stood beneath a large stage at the west end of the court.

I was breaking one of my mother's cardinal rules: I was attending the funeral of someone I'd never met. In my family, funeral-going (unless one had been so closely connected to the deceased that it was unavoidable) was considered almost indecent, a voyeuristic, vulgar indulgence in a vicarious emotion, an intrusion into the privacy of other people's lives (rather like entering someone's bedroom uninvited). Death (like sex) was not to be shared with strangers. In other words, we were afraid of dying.

"I can't go to that funeral," I'd told Richard.

"Why not?" he'd asked, surprised.

"Because I never met Dennis. I don't even know his mother."

"That doesn't matter."

"Well, of *course* it matters!"

"Not to the Apaches!" He'd laughed. "In San Carlos, in case you hadn't noticed, funerals are important events! Anyone can attend."

"Morbid," I'd muttered.

"Well, morbid or not, Dennis was my client, and everybody will think you're being disrespectful if you don't show up."

At that point, I hadn't cared what everybody else thought, but because of Richard, I'd relented and rummaged around in my closet for something that seemed suitably "funereal." Naturally, I'd overdressed. Everyone else, of course, looked cooler. In my dark skirt and jacket I felt, as usual, painfully conspicuous. But the worst part, the real reason for my discomfort, was the fact that the casket up at the front of the hall held the body of a nineteen-year-old kid.

Good Lord, I wondered, why not some octogenarian? Or someone who had led an unhealthy lifestyle? But Dennis Porter hadn't drunk alcohol or taken drugs. What happened to him could happen to anyone. He had died from leukemia that, undetected for weeks by the Indian Health Service doctors at the local hospital, had eventually been diagnosed by a private physician thirty miles away in the town of Globe.

"Dennis is terminal," the doctor had told Richard earlier. "He's got maybe a few months."

"I told that doctor I wish he hadn't been so specific," Richard said to me later. "I explained that Dennis had applied for a BIA scholarship for college to study criminology, which is what the poor kid had always wanted, but that I couldn't recommend him, knowing he was going to die."

"So what did the doctor say then?" I wanted to know.

"He told me to forget we'd ever talked." Richard laughed. "He promised to write something suitably vague on Dennis's medical report."

Before Dennis died, he finished almost two semesters at Eastern Arizona Junior College in Thatcher, and his mother, Johanna, was grateful to Richard for giving her son what he wanted during the last year of his life. She wanted Richard to take part in the funeral, and Father Bart, the Catholic priest, agreed. Dennis was not raised Catholic, but the pastor of the mission to which his family had belonged for generations refused to bury him.

"I haven't seen Dennis in church for years," the pastor reportedly said to Johanna. "This will be a good lesson."

"A lesson for Dennis?" I asked, sarcastically, when Richard told me about it. "It's a little late, isn't it? Anyway, what about Christian charity?"

"Don't worry, Johanna will show him," Richard promised. "You can count on it."

And she did. In defiance of her pastor, she had approached Father Bart at the Catholic mission.

"Who can know the mind of God, Johanna?" Father Bart had said.

"She'll send her boy off in fine style, after all," Richard said with satisfaction.

He'd certainly been right about that, I decided, as I realized the whole tribal council was assembled up front (Johanna's late husband had been a vice-chairman) along with a criminology professor to do the eulogy. The professor, a white man with a blond crew cut and wearing a light blue suit, stood at the microphone on the stage, saying good things about Dennis's courage and commitment and how he'd stayed in school even when he was very sick. "If Dennis had lived," the professor finished, "he would have made a fine policeman, which is all he ever wanted from the time he was a little boy."

Richard read from the Bible ("In my Father's house are many mansions"), and Father Bart, in his brown Franciscan habit, peered down through ancient rimless spectacles on the elegant bronze coffin covered with an enormous cascade of white and yellow gladioli and prayed that the angels would lead Dennis gently into paradise.

Then, row by row, led by the members of the tribal council (Stetsons held respectfully in their hands), we filed by Johanna, who was crumpled forward on her chair. With one hand she clutched her younger son, a boy of eleven or twelve, and with the other she reached out to shake hands with everyone who walked by. I barely touched her hand before walking quickly to the tall doors marked with the EXIT sign where Richard waited.

"Don't look so uptight," he whispered.

"I can't help it," I said. "I don't want to be here."

"Quiet," he said. "Someone might hear you."

"I don't care."

"Yes, you do."

"I don't."

"Let's go to Phoenix for the weekend," he said. "We can leave the kids with the grandmothers and go out to dinner." He smiled, persuasively.

"OK," I said, giving up. He knew those Phoenix weekends were my literal and figurative oases in the desert. Since our arrival the previous July at this dusty little outpost from which even Geronimo fled almost a century before, I'd felt caught between what I interpreted as muted hostility on the part of Native Americans and the obvious conservatism of the white government community that viewed Richard and me as "Chicago radicals," even though we'd grown up only one hundred miles from San Carlos. I had a hard time connecting with anyone.

"Well, you see, Ted Whitebull called this staff meeting before you got here," drawled my neighbor Irene in her Texas accent, "and he made out like Richard was some kind of Superman, the way he was going to come in here and *get things done*! Now, people don't like it when somebody just arrives and proceeds to upset the apple cart, do they?"

Although I didn't know what apple carts we'd upset, I could certainly see her point.

Where did we belong? Arizona was our home state and we'd wanted very much to come back, but since we'd returned I'd felt homesick for Chicago. Recently, I'd been attacked with bouts of nostalgia for people whose names I didn't know: the jazz flutist who walked down the sidewalk in the summertime, sending his high, lyric notes flickering like sunshine through green leaves into our open window; the red-haired Greek down on Halsted Street who passed out free glasses of ouzo to the customers waiting in line for a table in the restaurant at the back of his grocery store; the old black woman down at the main post office building who wrapped herself in an American flag on cold winter days.

I entertained fantasies of walking down Seventy-ninth Street, past the Rib Crib with huge slabs of barbecued pork turning on the rotisserie in the window, by the storefront churches named Solid Rock and Ark of Safety, to the Illinois Central station where the train carried me on weekends to the more elegant world of Marshall Field's and the Chicago Art Institute. But most of all, I longed for the Saturday morning Breadbasket meetings where Jesse Jackson's righteous anger, tempered by Ben Branch's mournful blues, created a community that welcomed even white liberals like Richard and me.

"You remember only the good things," Richard reminded me. "What about the times the boys got chased from the park by the kids with switchblades? And don't forget how Patrick turned over his milk money every day to that Blackstone Ranger crossing guard so he could get to kindergarten! A year ago you couldn't wait to get back to Arizona! I swear, you're never satisfied!"

He was right, of course. A year before, I was more than ready to leave that cold city with gray skies and no sun and come home to the mountains and desert. But it was not to be the homecoming I had envisioned. Exhilarated by the '60s (in that city of the '60s), I think we'd lost touch with the rest of the country. We naively expected reservation Native Americans to be as militant and radical as urban minorities. For example, while we thought of Geronimo as a hero to be resurrected into a rally cry for Indian rights, the Apaches we'd talked with seemed to view him as a renegade outlaw with whose actions they did not want to be associated.

I had marched in peace demonstrations in Chicago, and during the 1968 Democratic National Convention, Richard had been tear-gassed in Grant Park while protesting the war in Vietnam. Because American Indians, like blacks, Chicanos and poor whites, rarely got college deferments from the draft, thereby contributing far more than their share to the military system, we thought our actions would be to them a sign of solidarity, a common bond. But "hippies" many of them said when we talked about the peace movement—"draft dodgers."

It did not take long to discover that the Apaches took enormous pride in the members of their tribe who had served in the armed forces, from the army scouts of the late nineteenth century (eleven of whom were awarded the Medal of Honor) to the infantrymen of Vietnam. They had always fought with distinction. It was no coincidence that old Geronimo and his little band were the last American Indians to be rounded up and reserved. They had, after all, written the book on guerrilla warfare.

That first fall in San Carlos, we watched a Veterans Day parade that equaled, in patriotic fervor, any of Mayor Daley's State Street pageants. Above the horses—colorful pintos and spotted Appaloosas—above the bands and the costumed schoolchildren and Miss San Carlos in her fringed and beaded buckskin dress, high above all that on a mesa overlooking the town, flew flags, dozens of flags, standard size, government issue, American flags, red and white against the blue November sky. They flew from flagpoles over graves of Apache warriors who had fought for the United States.

Outside Burdette Hall in the big dirt parking lot, Richard and I waited while it seemed that most of San Carlos poured out of the gymnasium. In front of the building, an air force F-86 fighter jet stood on a pedestal mounted in cement, looking like a gigantic toy model. What was a fighter plane doing here, I wondered, one hundred miles from any of the Arizona air bases? The sun glinted sharply off its wings. Reaching into my purse for dark glasses, I quickly slipped them on, grateful for the partial barrier they provided between me and the rest of the crowd.

A man standing next to me drank from a can of strawberry soda pop. He wore Levi's stiff with dirt, a cowboy shirt that might once have been green and a bright yellow hard hat that matched his eyes. A red, white and blue plastic rosary, the kind given away free at the Catholic mission, hung around his neck. A few black hairs, five or six inches long, sprouted incongruously from each side of his mouth and wound down around his chin, giving him the look of an oriental cat. He smiled at me with yellow teeth. "God bless you, Mr. David!" he said, lurching across me to grab Richard's hand. He smelled of bonfires, booze and sweat.

"He smelled of funeral wakes," Richard told me later. "They last for days, sometimes a week, and of course, when it's cold they all stand around a bonfire."

"God bless you, Mr. David," the man said, again. "Have you got a dollar?"

Several people turned and grinned at us.

"Nope," said Richard.

"How about fifty cents?"

Richard dug into his pocket, found a quarter, some dimes, and handed them to the man.

"God bless you, Mr. David, Richard, Sir," the man said jovially, pumping Richard's hand. "This your wife?" He smiled upon me benevolently. "So glad to meet you, Missus." He grabbed my hand. "Richard here is my best friend."

He slipped the patriotic rosary over his head and dangled it in front of my face. "You can have it for a dollar."

"No, thanks." I smiled. I couldn't help it.

"Seventy-five cents? How 'bout fifty cents?" he tried again, his own smile dazzling.

"Goodbye, Benjamin," said Richard. "Stay away from the bootleggers."

"I don't go to no bootleggers, Richard," Benjamin said piously. He tipped his hard hat with exaggerated gallantry and walked away.

"Friend of yours?" I whispered.

"My *best* friend. You heard the man." He smiled and turned back toward Burdette Hall. The tall doors of the gymnasium opened once again, and there was Dennis's coffin, not wheeled on some mortuary apparatus but carried by his friends. Shyly, they stood there for a moment, the eight of them, just boys in Levi's and cowboy boots, their black hair shining brightly in the sunlight. Then, they laughed softly among themselves—Johanna, behind them, smiled!—as they juggled their burden into the hearse. That sweet act, plain and simple, startled me and made me catch my breath. I remembered looking at my father in his heavy bronze casket, touching my fingers to flesh too hard and pink in the false, rosy glow of the electric mortuary lamp, not really believing, not then, not for years afterward, that he was dead. But these boys who carried their friend, these boys who'd watched him die for most of a year, seemed at ease with their awful task, went about it as naturally as they would later shoot baskets from the court that for a brief time had served as a funeral chapel.

I was struck by the Apache at the front of the coffin. Like the others, he wore cowboy boots and faded Levi's, but his black, knee length Edwardian frock coat and long hair made him resemble the chiefs of the 1880s who had traveled to Washington, D.C., to meet the President.

"Who's that splendid looking guy at the front?" I asked.

"The kid dressed up like a Beatle?"

"Yes, that one."

"That's David Houzous," Richard said.

"He looks like some old-time chief."

"Well, he comes by it naturally," Richard told me. "He's a cousin of Geronimo."

"Geronimo? The *real* Geronimo?"

"Yup, the real Geronimo."

"No kidding!"

"No kidding," Richard said. "David's related to him on his father's side."

"I'm surprised he admits it," I said. "I thought everyone around here was ashamed of the old warrior. They think he's a criminal."

"Not this family."

I watched David Houzous and thought of shadowy tintypes and sepia Curtis photographs. I saw Geronimo, the last Apache to surrender, running deer-like all over southern Arizona and northern Sonora, confusing the cavalry, the Mexican army, illusive for years in the Sierra Madre, embodied there, that minute, in his young relative.

And that was the moment I got hooked for good.

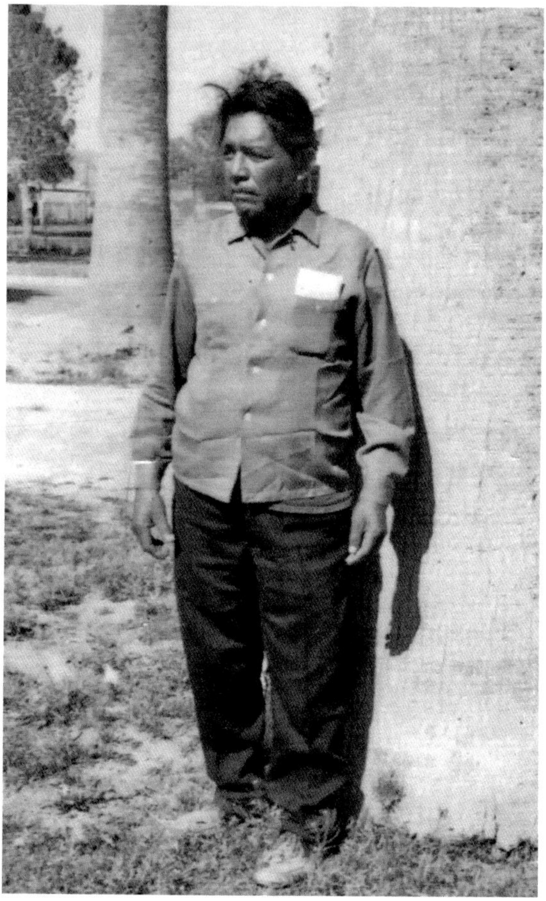

Benjamin.

Benjamin

My daddy's dead, Richard," Benjamin said. "Please give me fifty dollars to go to his funeral."

"I'll drive you to Phoenix, Benjamin, and it won't cost you fifty dollars," Richard told him.

"Daddy" was not Benjamin's father, nor was he an Apache, and his death ended what was surely a bizarre relationship. "The Major," as he wanted everyone to call him, was a former military man who kept his title even after entering the U.S. Civil Service. He stood perhaps six feet, three inches tall and weighed around two hundred pounds. Although his perfectly groomed gray hair and arrogant swagger would have done credit to an Englishman of the East India Company during the Raj, I think he preferred to think of himself as Wyatt Earp. He drove around the reservation in his Jeep with a canvas top, antenna whipping in the wind, rifle displayed prominently in the back. In one pocket he carried a flask of Chivas Regal and in the other, a can of mace. He often scared the nurses in the Indian Health compound by shooting wax bullets at a life-sized figure of a man painted on one wall of his twelve- by ten-foot apartment where he lived during the week. On weekends, he went home to his wife in North Phoenix. He liked to play classical records at the tribal radio station he had set up to "give the Indians a little culture"—or "cultch," as he said.

Technically, the Major, who had been in San Carlos for years, was BIA Superintendent Whitebull's administrative assistant, but a lot of people (both Apache and white) believed he held more power than the superintendent.

When the special FBI agent assigned to the tribal police resigned, the Major literally took over the police station. He brought that off by aligning himself with the current tribal chairman's political organization.

The Major possessed a remarkable network of informants, the most loyal of whom was Benjamin. In return for whiskey (not Chivas Regal) and money, Benjamin gave excellent tips that often led to arrests for serious crimes. Benjamin had his limits, though; he never ratted on murderers. The risks were too great.

The Major boasted he was not without compassion: he knew whom to arrest and throw in jail during holidays and cold weather. For example, he could always depend on Benjamin to cook the jail turkeys for Thanksgiving and Christmas.

Inevitably, the Major abused his power to such a degree that the tribal police complained to the superintendent, who got him transferred to another reservation in Arizona. A year later, he rolled his Jeep and was killed instantly. It was several days after the Major's death that Benjamin had come to Richard to ask for money.

"When's the funeral?" Richard asked. "Tomorrow morning," Benjamin blubbered, "but you don't have to drive me. If you'll just give me money…"

"Come on," Richard said. "Let's get going. You can stay overnight and come home on the bus tomorrow afternoon."

When Richard and Benjamin arrived that afternoon at the Bethany Home Chapel and Mortuary in North Phoenix, they were confronted at the door by an elegantly dressed and coiffed receptionist.

"I want to see my daddy!" wailed Benjamin.

"I think perhaps you've come to the wrong place," replied the receptionist, clearly aghast at the sight of Benjamin.

"I want to see my daddy!" Benjamin repeated. "My daddy, the Major."

"*Your* daddy? The Major is *your* daddy?" she asked.

"My daddy, yes! And I want to say goodbye."

"I'm afraid," she replied, "the Major is not yet ready to receive visitors."

"The receptionist's face," Richard said later, "was worth the trip to Phoenix."

Richard gave Benjamin money to stay the night in the old, but very nice, San Carlos hotel downtown. He also gave him, along with a clearly marked bus schedule, enough cash to go back to the mortuary the following morning and to return to the reservation. Thirty minutes after Richard arrived home that day, our telephone rang. It was Benjamin calling from the Peridot Trading Post.

"I just left you in Phoenix!" Richard said. "Why are you here?"

"I decided not to stay for the funeral," Benjamin said, cheerfully.

"Why on earth not?" Richard asked, stunned.

"Well, Mr. David, sir, I want to remember him like he was."

"Benjamin finally got you, Mr. David," Richard's secretary, Joanne Thompson, said when he told her the story the next day. And for weeks afterward, when Richard walked down the hall at work, he was greeted by people snickering and saying, "I want to remember him like he was."

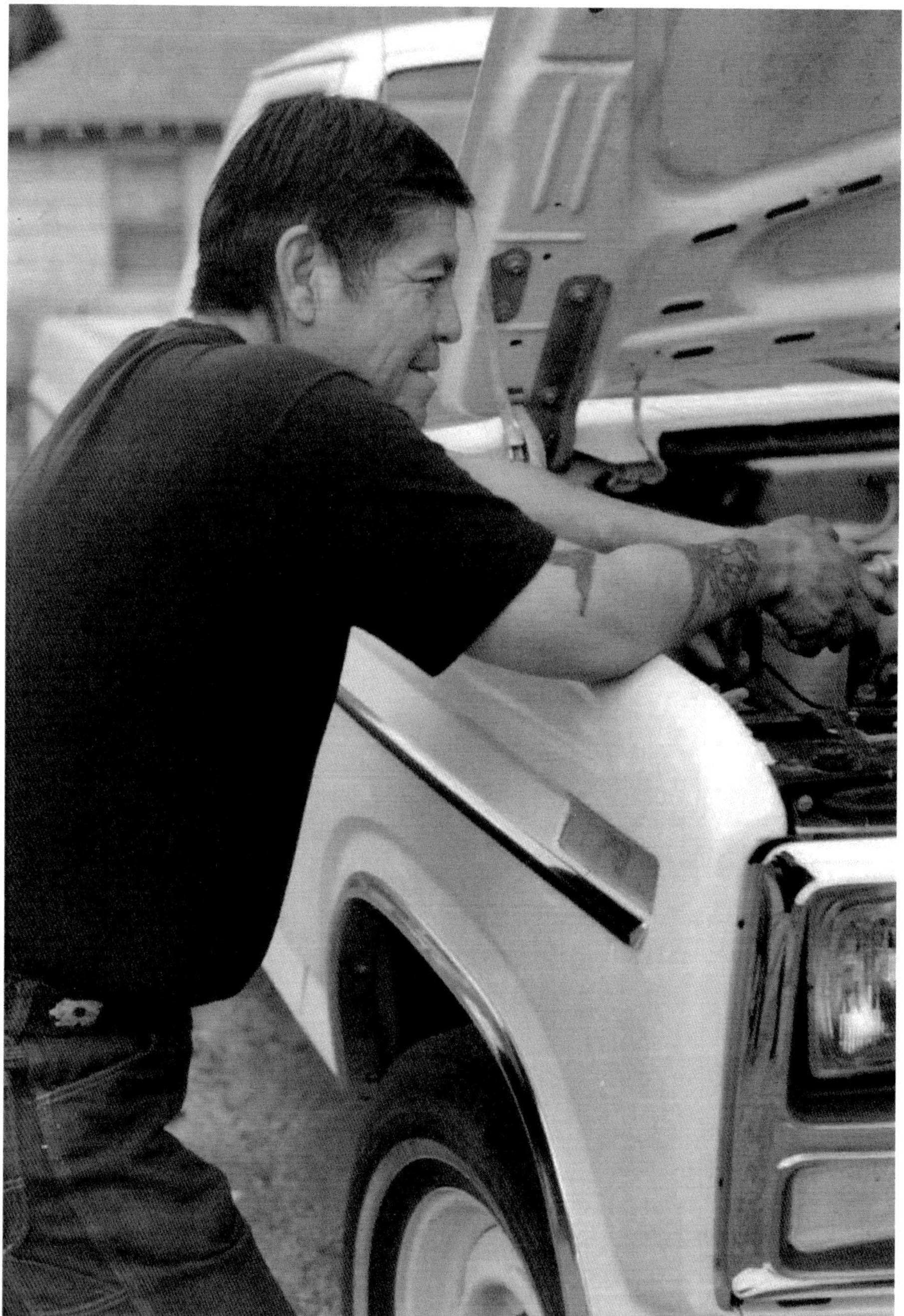

Ambrose Hoffman works on his beloved pickup truck in which he brought us the beautiful Scotch pine Christmas tree.

The Visit

The most beautiful Christmas tree of my life was a gift from the Apache Ambrose Hoffman. The year was 1973, and by that time we were living in one of the old stone houses. About two weeks before Christmas, Ambrose went up to the northern part of the reservation and cut a Scotch pine. That tree must have been thirteen feet tall because it nearly reached the ceiling. It was perfectly formed, absolutely fresh and we kept it up, I swear, until Lent. But I get ahead of myself. I mention the Christmas tree only because it is linked forever in my mind with one of the kindest men I have ever met.

Richard and I had known Ambrose and his wife, Linda, as long as we had known any Apaches in San Carlos. We met them at the Catholic mission when we first came to the reservation. They were the first adult Apaches to befriend us. Although our shared wedding anniversary date, December 27, the feast of St. John the Apostle, appeared to be the only thing we had in common, our friendship grew quickly and easily. Ambrose and Linda often walked to our house in the evening "just to visit" as they said. Occasionally, Linda would show us her beadwork necklaces and hair clasps—turquoise thunderbirds, yellow and orange sunbursts—which we purchased. But what they really came for was to fill us in on the latest reservation gossip, especially about politics. They loved to talk politics, both tribal and national. Ambrose did not like draft dodgers.

"I served in the United States Navy," he would occasionally remind us when we talked about our peace demonstrations in Chicago. "In the Korean conflict. With pride."

Ambrose wore his hair as if he were still in the navy—not a crew cut, but very short. "High and tight" is the military term. He dressed in Levi's and a blue chambray work shirt. Linda wore cotton print dresses and loafers with white socks. Her hair was always pulled into a bun at the back of her neck.

Ambrose and Linda had one child, a son named Sammy, who worked at Motorola in Phoenix. Sammy was married and would soon give them grandchildren. I know they looked forward to that because they truly liked children. They liked ours. Ambrose teased the boys, especially Christopher, who was as round and deceptively cherubic as Ambrose himself. And Linda loved Noelle. She taught her Apache words. For the first five years of her life, until she attended kindergarten in Colorado, Noelle spoke with an Apache accent.

"That First Noelle sure talks Apache," Linda said one evening. She spoke to Noelle, and Noelle babbled back.

"See? I say, 'Hi, how you doing?' And she say, 'Hi, how you doing, too?'"

"*Shiime' shiime'*, " Linda said. My baby, my baby.

"*Shiime'*," Noelle said.

"*Gidi goliinii*." Linda pointed to our cat and laughed. "*Gidi goliinii*!" Wildcat.

"*Gidi gidi*," Noelle said, pulling the cat's tail.

"You talk good Apache, Baby." Linda giggled.

I always loved their visits, but there was one day during our second year in San Carlos when I was especially grateful for their presence.

Although Richard and I would form some of our most enduring friendships with two families in the Indian Health Service, one of my early visits to the Indian Health compound was not auspicious. I had been invited to a coffee to meet the wives of three new doctors. These doctors, like their counterparts on every reservation in America, had recently arrived for two years, an assignment that would prevent them from going to Vietnam.

After Patrick and Christopher left for school, I put Noelle in the stroller, made my way across the cattle guard, entered the fenced area that separated the Indian Health compound from the rest of San Carlos and walked down a street where identical stucco houses were planted in rows. When I arrived, I was introduced to the three women. The first one seemed quite friendly. She was an artist from California, from the Bay Area, she said, and she laughed when she told us that before she'd come to Arizona, she'd imagined she would be so close to Santa Fe that she could just run right up there and meet Georgia O'Keeffe! The second one, a woman with a spiky blonde crew cut and little wire-rimmed glasses, was not so friendly. Not only was she a doctor's wife but she was a doctor, as well. Right after she made that point clear, she asked me what my husband did. As I sat down and settled Noelle on my lap, I told her that Richard directed the employment program for the Bureau of Indian Affairs. Crew Cut glared at me through her little round glasses.

"I don't suppose you work," she said.

"No," I said, irritated by her comment. She clearly did not consider raising children work, but then, just as clearly, she'd never tried it.

Noelle reached up, pulled the gold hoop earring out of my ear and poked it in my nose. Everyone but Crew Cut laughed. I took the earring away from Noelle and tried to interest her in the long string of beads around my neck. She was more interested in my cup of coffee. I put it down on the floor next to my chair. She began to play with the zipper on the front of my dress.

"Where are you from?" the third wife asked. She had long black hair held back on one side with a clip. "Where did you go to school?" I told her that my husband and I had grown up in Chandler, a little town near Phoenix, and that we'd graduated from Arizona State University. I asked her where she was from.

"New York," she said. And then she said, she really did, "But I don't suppose you've ever been there."

"I *have* been to New York…"

"We've been in Cambridge for the past four years," she interrupted. "My husband graduated from Harvard Medical School, of course."

Of course?

And that's how it went: where did you go to school and what do you do. And finally, where can we go to get out of here? Santa Fe, of course, and even Tucson might be a possibility. But Phoenix? What was there in Phoenix?

The conversation drifted around me, and I wondered how soon I could make a graceful exit. Sooner than I thought, it turned out. But it was not graceful.

"Oh, my goodness!" Someone said. "Good heavens!" I looked around to see what was wrong and realized everyone was staring at *me*. I glanced down to see my dress gaping open; Noelle had unzipped it all the way down to my waist. The doctors' wives watched in silence as I juggled Noelle with one hand and grabbed the zipper with the other and tugged. It jammed on the facing. Furiously, I plopped Noelle down on the floor, yanked on the zipper and zipped myself back up. Then I picked up Noelle, thanked my hostess for inviting me and left.

When we arrived home, Ambrose and Linda were on my doorstep. I had never been so glad to see them.

"Hi," Ambrose said. "We thought you would be back soon so we just decided to wait." I opened the front door, and they followed me inside. Would they like some iced tea? They would.

"Hi, First Noelle!" Linda giggled. Ambrose laughed as if he hadn't heard his wife say that many times. Noelle reached her arms up to Linda and grabbed her hair, tearing it loose from the bun.

"Hey, cut it out, *Baby*!" Linda laughed as she carefully disentangled her hair and placed Noelle on her lap. I brought out the iced tea, and we settled around the table. I told them I had just met the wives of the three new doctors.

"Draft dodgers," Ambrose said. "They come here and *practice* on us for two years just to get out of going to Vietnam."

"Oh, well, I guess they're good doctors, anyway," I said. I was tired of doctors and their wives, and I was certainly tired of arguing with Ambrose about Vietnam.

"You know that new kid?" Ambrose grinned.

"What new kid?"

"Doctor *Haaarvard*," he said dramatically.

"I met his wife today," I told him, still mortified by my quite literal exposure to the new residents of the Indian Health compound.

"He sure does not know how to deliver babies," Ambrose said. I looked at Ambrose skeptically. The Apaches were full of stories about the "young docs" who "practiced" on the Indians. But a Harvard Medical School graduate who didn't know how to deliver babies?

"It's *true*!" Ambrose said.

"He got real mixed up when he was supposed to deliver a baby the other night," Linda said.

"He did not know what to do," Ambrose said. "He got real *scared*!"

"Are you serious?"

"I am *sure* serious!" Ambrose said. "The nurse yelled at him, 'What the hell you guys learn in medical school these days?' That nurse, you know, she weighs maybe two hundred pounds, she shoved little Doctor Harvard out of the way and she delivered that baby *herself*! And now they are sending him down to Phoenix Indian Hospital, and he does not get to do anything but deliver babies for a whole month!" Ambrose lifted his chin and pointed his lips in the general direction of Phoenix. "*One whole month*!"

"*One whole month*!" Linda chimed in.

Ambrose smiled at me, and I laughed. He had banished my humiliation with three words. Three words. Just like that. He was a magician, and I wanted to hug him, wanted to give him a great big bear hug, but I did not dare. He would have been mortified.

HAIR

March 19, 1890
The Commissioner of Indian Affairs banned Native American religious ceremonies. He ordered Native Americans to change their names, to dress as white men, and to cut off their hair. The penalty for refusing to conform would be severe.[*]

In 1837 the State of Chihuahua [Mexico] *offered a bounty of 100 pesos for Apache warriors' scalps, 50 pesos for females' scalps, and 25 for children. Many unscrupulous white men found butchering Apaches more profitable than seeking gold in this barren county.*[†]

Esther Goode, shining hair pulled tightly back from her elegant face, magenta blouse glowing against her flawless brown skin, stood in our living room next to her fourteen-year-old brother, Eldad, arguing. "I just thought you would cut it for him! I didn't think you would make some big deal out of it." She dropped the lids of her almond eyes.

"Eldad," asked Richard. "Do you want your hair cut off?"

Eldad's shoulder-length black hair fell forward as he stared at the floor and shook his head.

---

*. Virginia Cole Trenholm, *The Arapahoes, Our People* (Norman: University of Oklahoma Press, 1986), 280–81.

†. Mike Flanagan, "Out West," *Empire Magazine, Denver Post*, September 18, 1983.

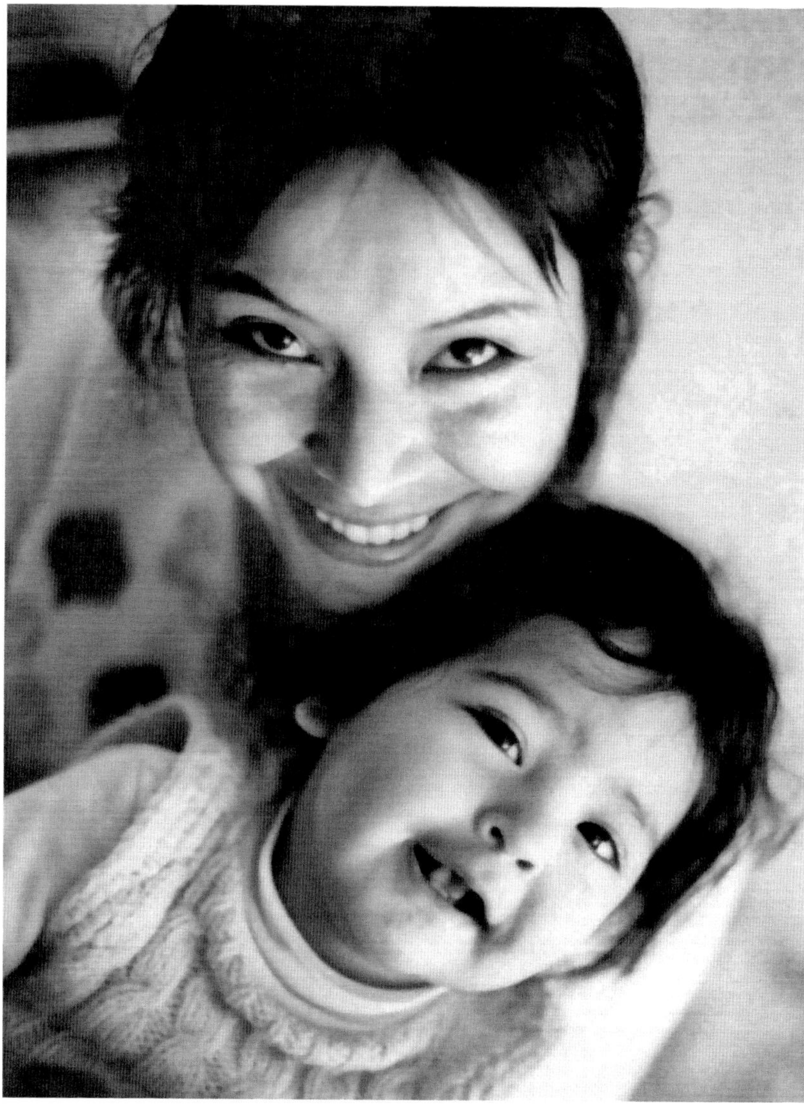

Esther Goode with her daughter, Jessica. *Photo by Jerry Melore.*

"So why should he have to cut it?" Richard asked. "I don't think they can keep him out of a public school because of the length of his hair."

"You don't know Globe High School," Esther retorted, opening her eyes wide. "Apaches get treated like dirt. Look at Eldad!" She gestured with one hand. "You think he's some kind of hippie protester? He's just a little kid. They'll make it really hard on him if he doesn't do what they say."

"And they told Eldad he would be suspended if he didn't cut off his hair?"

Esther reached into the pocket of her Levi's, pulled out a piece of paper and handed it to Richard. He unfolded the paper and read in silence.

I felt a quick surge of anticipation, and not only at the prospect of a good fight; I suddenly felt less isolated. We'd been in San Carlos for over a year, and other than Raleigh and Ralph who came to repair things, and Ambrose and Linda, Esther Goode was the first Apache adult to come knocking on our door.

Eldad, thin and bony faced, looked up at Richard. His shoulders, outlined beneath his skimpy white T-shirt, seemed small and vulnerable. Except for his twelve-year-old sister, Mariam, he was the youngest of a dozen or so kids, all of whom but the two or three eldest were crammed, along with a couple of their little nieces, into a two-bedroom trailer. Their father, Britton Goode, the old medicine man, struggled to hold his family together. Their mother, Marie, had been killed the year before when her car stalled on the tracks of an approaching train.

"You know," Richard said, "I'm sure this is illegal. I can't believe that, in 1971, hair is still an issue. Before you decide to do anything, let me check around."

Esther looked not altogether convinced. Although she stood at least two feet from Eldad—Apaches seldom touch each other in a casual way—she exuded maternal protection.

"Look," Richard reassured her, "if I find that nothing can be done, I'll cut Eldad's hair. OK?"

She pushed out her lip. "Yeah. Sure."

But the events of the next few days, as Richard recounted them to me every evening after work, were hardly encouraging. When Richard sought the advice of an Apache social worker with the Bureau of Indian Affairs, she told him to "stay out of it. We've worked too hard to overcome our bad image. What you're trying to do is none of your business."

"It's Eldad who doesn't want to cut his hair; it's not my idea," Richard defended himself. "If he wants to wear it long, what difference does it make?"

"If he causes trouble it will reflect back on the whole tribe," the social worker warned.

"How will Eldad cause trouble just by wearing his hair long?" Richard asked.

"By not obeying the school rules," the social worker said.

"But why have those rules?" Richard persisted. "Why is it the school's business how people wear their hair?" The social worker looked at him as if he were crazy.

"Listen, Señor, I admire what you're doing," said the BIA education director. The Chicano himself had graduated from Globe High School.

"But when you're in the minority at that school, you learn to play their game if you ever want to get anywhere."

"You don't think we should push it, then?"

"Richard," said Cruz gently, "when I was a kid I would get spanked whenever I forgot and spoke Spanish on the playground."

Richard, disheartened, took Christopher for a walk one evening and ran into the tall, skinny man from Louisiana who worked with the BIA Social Services.

"Well, look, man," said Jim Foxx, after Richard told him how frustrated he felt. "Why don't you quit listening to all this damn advice and go ahead and do what you think is right?"

The following morning, Richard called the high school principal.

"You Eldad's attorney?" the principal asked, sarcastically. "You don't like it, you can sue us."

"OK," Richard said, banging down the telephone. But when he drove down to Tucson to enlist the help of the American Civil Liberties Union, he was told they already had a "hair case"—a white student down in Bisbee, a town near the Mexican border. Richard argued that Eldad's situation was different, that it was probably racial, but the ACLU didn't see it that way. As far as they were concerned, they had one hair case and they weren't interested in another.

Before Richard left Tucson, he went to the *Arizona Daily Star* and talked to a young reporter named Joel Nilsson who'd just returned from the Peace Corps. Unlike the ACLU, Joel was so interested that he drove up to San Carlos and Globe, where he spent the day interviewing anyone who would talk to him. He ended up at our house for dinner, and that night, he slept on the couch in our living room.

"You've got to meet Billie Shoecraft," Joel told us with an amused look.

"Who's Billie Shoecraft?" Richard asked.

"She and her husband, Willard, own the Globe radio station that broadcasts the *Apache Hour*," Joel said. "Billie and Willard have a fourteen-year-old year son named Robert. Apparently, when Robert heard about what happened to Eldad, he marched defiantly into the principal's office, pulled his blond curls down to his shoulders and announced that if Eldad Goode was going to be expelled from school they'd have to kick him out, too."

"What happened?" I asked.

"Well, the principal really didn't have any choice, did he?" Joel said. "Poor principal." He smiled. "I don't think it will be long before you meet Billie Shoecraft."

Joel was right.

"Well, dang it," the woman snorted as she told us of her telephone conversation with the tribal attorneys in Phoenix. "What the hell did they mean they're retained to represent the tribe as a whole and not individual members?"

I stared at Billie Shoecraft. She stood five feet tall and weighed no more than ninety-five pounds. She had platinum hair and wore four-inch heels and what looked like a Rudi Gernreich mini-dress; she dripped with a couple of old pawn squash blossom necklaces, four or five turquoise rings and at least five bracelets. She'd called Richard on the afternoon of September 22, the day that Joel's article "Apache Youth in Globe Claims Discrimination" appeared in the *Daily Star*, and they'd arranged to meet.

"I told those guys," Billie went on, "that what affects this one little kid affects the whole tribe! I also told them I could damn well afford to have my own attorney represent Eldad as well as my own son, but that they had a moral obligation to get off their butts and do it themselves."

One of the tribal attorneys, Phil Shea, did feel a "moral obligation." He offered to take the case pro bono, and a few days later, he called Richard from Phoenix to say he had a restraining order from the Superior Court of Gila County. The order called the school administration's action a deprivation of Eldad's due process of law, which was guaranteed by the Fourteenth Amendment of the United States Constitution and by Article II, Section 4 of the Arizona Constitution.

"This restraining order will get Eldad back in school until the hearing," Phil told him. "I have to be in court tomorrow morning, but if you want to deliver it…"

"I'll be down in two hours to pick it up," Richard promised.

"Do you want to ride along?" Richard asked me the following morning as he prepared to deliver both Eldad and the restraining order to Globe High School.

"I wouldn't miss it," I said, feeling as if I were back in Chicago on the picket line. We drove the twenty-five miles from San Carlos to Globe where Richard parked the government car with a flourish in a no-parking zone directly in front of the old high school. The autumn air was warm and hazy, and a tiny breeze lifted a strand of Eldad's hair and curled it around his cheek. As we walked up the impossibly steep flight of broad stone steps, I wondered if he felt as nervous as I did. My hands were cold and wet and my stomach lurched, and all I had to do was watch while Eldad took the heat. I'd never felt this frightened marching down State Street, not even in front of the Chicago Police. Of course, then there'd been hundreds of us; today we were only three.

The principal turned in his swivel chair to face us. *Why, he actually has a red neck!* I thought, startled. *Or he would if he had a neck!* His round head, red and bald, sat directly on his shoulders. An enormous stomach bulged over his belt. His giant hands, fingers splayed, pushed down on the desk before him.

"You say you got what there?" he growled, taking the restraining order from Richard's hand.

"This copy is yours," Richard said. "The original is on file at the Gila County Courthouse." The principal stared at the piece of paper.

"You'll be notified as to the date of the hearing," Richard continued.

The principal glared at Richard.

"Your suggestion," Richard reminded him, softly. "All I wanted was Eldad back in school."

"Get to class. *Boy*." The principal waved us away and began shuffling papers on his desk.

I opened my mouth, but I saw Richard's warning glance. I compressed my lips and did not call the principal a jerk.

The passing bell rang as we left the office, and the hall filled quickly with chattering, yelling students who suddenly turned silent the instant they saw Eldad.

As he walked toward his locker alone, he looked like a shy, small bird that had stumbled into a nest of vultures. *Oh, God*, I thought, my stomach tightening, *maybe we shouldn't have interfered!* What if things went harder on him now than if he *had* cut off his hair? Maybe these kids hated Apaches as much as generations of Globe residents before them.

A Chicano kid with a black mustache stared at Eldad. The kid's biceps bulged from a black T-shirt printed with a picture of Cesar Chavez and the words VIVA LA HUELGA in Day-Glo orange. The Chicano nodded solemnly, raised one clenched fist in the air and punched Eldad's shoulder, gently, with the other.

I sighed in relief as Eldad stuck out his chin and walked off down the hall.

The hearing itself was historical in that it was, I believe, one of the first times that Apaches and whites had joined forces in court. But aside from this remarkable fact, the three days in the courtroom seemed, at times, more comic than serious. At one point, the judge had to declare a recess because of the noise from a school band marching by the courthouse.

"Who's that little kid in the convertible?" I asked Cruz Salas, who was standing next to me on the courthouse steps.

"That," replied Cruz proudly, "is the new NFL Punt, Pass and Kick champion. He won the national title last week in Dallas. He goes to school with my kid at Holy Angels Elementary."

The boy sat triumphantly on the back of the car. His heavy hair swung like a curtain and grazed his shoulders as he turned from side to side, waving at the cheering crowd. I wondered if he would be forced to cut off his hair when he got to Globe High School.

Following the recess, the Globe School Board presented a perfectly coiffed white social worker who stated that dress and hair codes were important means of discipline. (I thought with irony of the Indian social worker who agreed, and I was relieved that the school attorneys had not had the foresight to interview her and call her to the witness stand.) Their second witness was an "expert" from some teachers' college in Fresno, California, who admitted under Phil Shea's cross-examination that, yes, he regularly supplemented his income by testifying at "hair and dress code trials" in various states, in return for expenses and one hundred dollars a day.

"So, in a sense, what you are," said Phil gleefully, "is a sort of educational prostitute. Is that correct?"

Startled, the witness turned to appeal to the judge who sustained the school attorney's objection even as he shouted it.

But they were no match, those two witnesses, for Esther, who coolly told the judge that, yes, her father had once been a medicine man and that she and her brother Eldad followed traditional Apache ways, or for Tony Machukay from the Arizona Indian Commission, who explained that, among Apaches, long hair had always been, quite simply, a symbol of manhood. Even Eldad, whose natural reticence, we'd feared, might come across on the witness stand as sullenness, presented an almost prototypical picture of old Apache stoicism, complementing perfectly the witty sophistication of Billie Shoecraft's son.

The favorable outcome of the hearing, even before the ACLU case, formed a precedent for public schools in the state of Arizona.

Elated, we stood on the steps of the courthouse after the judge read his opinion.

"Well, we did it," said Richard with satisfaction.

"We *screwed* those bastards," agreed Billie Shoecraft.

Later that year, around Christmas, Richard opened our front door to see Cruz Salas wearing an enormous sombrero, a charro hat from Guadalajara, embroidered in blue and red silk thread and decorated with green sequins.

"Who are you? Pancho Villa?" I asked when Cruz strolled into the living room.

"*Please*!" Cruz protested. "Don't say that. I will explain. My grandfather brought this hat from Mexico during the revolution."

"Oh, it's a family heirloom," I said, impressed.

"My grandfather played in the town band. He played the tuba. When the revolutionaries came to town, the band played. When the Federalist soldiers came to town, the band played, also. When Pancho Villa discovered they played for both sides, he lined the band members up and shot the even-numbered ones. My grandfather, fortunately, was an odd number. Nevertheless, he stood there shaking in his tuba. My mother, who was a little girl holding tightly to my grandmother's hand, watched and told me all about it many years later. That day, my grandfather decided he would be a hell of a lot better off working in the mines of Arizona than playing in a band in Guadalajara." Cruz smiled. "And he was right."

"That's quite a story," Richard said.

"It's a true story." Cruz removed the sombrero and put it on Richard's head. "Permit me, Señor, to give you my grandfather's hat."

"*What?*" Richard said. "Don't be crazy! You can't give away your grandfather's hat!" He started to take off the sombrero.

"I certainly can," Cruz said, reaching out to stop him.

"But *why*?"

"Because, Amigo," Cruz said, "you have done something at Globe High School that many of us have wanted to do for a long, long time."

Richard, the ties from the hat dangling beneath his chin, looked down at the floor and then up, again, at Cruz.

"Cruz, I thank you and I'm honored, but…"

"Señor…"

"I can't accept it, Cruz…"

"I assure you, Ricardo," Cruz replied, no longer smiling as he grasped Richard by the elbow and shoulder. "I will be insulted if you do not."

On Christmas Day, Richard and I stood in Britton Goode's trailer drinking eggnog. Unaccustomed to swigging anything alcoholic at ten o'clock in the morning, I had to admit the holiday had taken on a singular brightness. I began to wonder how I would ever make it home to cook turkey for ten people that afternoon.

Eldad, uncharacteristically verbal, praised Richard's new red sweater. "I like that sweater a lot," he said, clearly hinting. "I sure *do like it*!"

"And I sure am sorry that I can't give you the sweater," Richard replied. "But I can't, because my mother-in-law made it for me for Christmas."

"Your mother-in-law?" Britton shrieked. He reached beneath his scarecrow hat to turn up his hearing aid. It squawked. He nodded, satisfied. "You say your mother-in-law made you that sweater?"

"That's what I said," Richard replied, facing Britton and speaking slowly. "My mother-in-law."

"Sure hope you didn't look at her face!" Britton yelled.

"Of *course* I looked at her face!"

"You know better than that, Richard!" Britton bellowed. "Bad *luck* if you look at your mother-in-law's *face*!"

"I'm not an Apache, Britton," Richard yelled back.

"That don't matter, Richard!"

Suddenly I felt my knees bend, and I found myself plopped down on the couch next to Esther.

"Richard, my true friend," said Eldad, with surprising eloquence. "Did I ever thank you for not cutting my hair?"

Esther and I looked at each other and giggled. I'd known, of course, soon after the hearing, that if Esther had really wanted her brother's hair cut short she would have done it herself. What she couldn't do herself was take on the Globe School Board. But the Chicago hippies could. Somehow, as Apaches often did, she'd intuitively sensed the truth: that Richard David had never in his life turned down a good crusade.

"Did I?" Eldad repeated.

"Did you what?"

"Thank you for not cutting my hair?"

"Oh, of course," Richard lied. "Many times! Don't you remember?"

"I sure like that *sweater*!" Eldad beamed with Christmas cheer. He put his arm across Richard's shoulder and smiled expansively around the room.

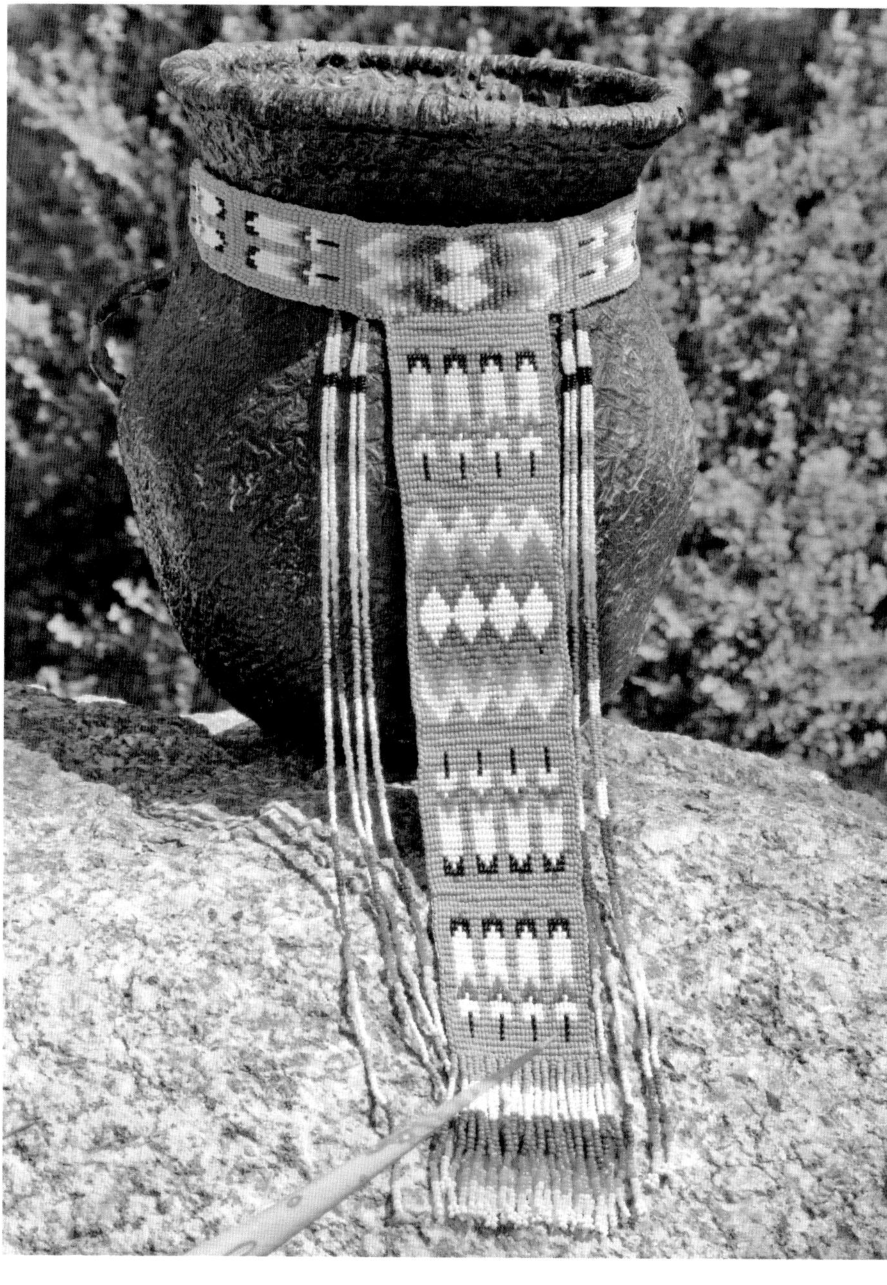

The T necklace, made by Martha Machukay, is the kind worn by a young woman at her Sunrise Ceremony.

Journal Notes, 1970–72

Sunrise Ceremony

"Dust! I love it!" the schoolteacher Nancy Chase cries, as her lean body bobs up and down in the line of mostly Apache dancers. Her long blonde hair swirls in the light from the bonfire as she throws her head back and laughs. This is not new to Nancy. Her father has worked for the Bureau of Indian Affairs for years, and she's grown up here at San Carlos.

On my left Richard is wheezing—his asthma does *not* love dust!—and on my right Mae, an older Apache woman, grins up at me. Her gray hair is in tiny braids all the way around her face, and her camp dress drags on the ground.

"Far out!" yells our friend Larry Barker at the other end of the line. His feet stomp back and forth to the drumbeat. His wife, Wendy, blinks her eyes against her contact lenses, and she laughs as tears stream down her pretty face. Larry and Wendy are visiting us from Berkeley, California, and I can tell from looking at them they can hardly believe the kind of experience we're providing. We're not providing the experience at all, of course. We are fortunate that their visit coincided with a Sunrise Ceremony, the most important, most sacred ritual to the Apaches, and that we have been invited to attend.

The Sunrise Ceremony is the four-day puberty rite for a girl who will now become not only a woman but also, for these four days, according to Apache tradition, she will be Changing Woman, the original Apache. The new woman dances, silently, alone, resplendent in a beaded buckskin dress, the fringe tinkling with tin cones. Her hair is decorated with eagle plumes, and her face is anointed with sacred yellow pollen.

The singers, men across the fire from us, chant the woman's way to beauty and harmony. She will never have menstrual cramps (I would love to have had this ceremony done for me!), and in happiness and fulfillment she will bear healthy children. Or at least that's what Esther Goode tells me. Esther did not have a Sunrise Ceremony because by the time she reached puberty, her parents had joined an evangelical church where they were told to give up their "devilish" Apache ways. Esther has always regretted this. She feels incomplete, somehow, she says. Something important is missing. It is especially painful to her, I think, because before her father followed her mother into the evangelical mission, he was a medicine man.

Why do some Christians feel they have the right to interfere with Native American religion? Why do they call it devil worship? These Christians say they are saving the souls of the Apaches, but I wonder. What kind of damage might they be doing to Native American psyches?

CATTLEMEN AND TRADERS

The San Carlos Reservation, with its five cattle associations, is Arizona's largest cattle ranch. We live on open rangeland. Cattle guards, steel grids composed of widely spaced transverse rods and rails, are installed on access roads in various places in order to prevent cattle from roaming around town. The cattle were not always owned by Apaches, as they are today.

"My uncle, John Osborn, came out in 1904 from Kansas on horseback to Old San Carlos, where San Carlos Lake is now, to be the foreman of the Aztec Land and Cattle Company," Joyce Montgomery, the trader, says. "The Aztec, which was formed by the Santa Fe Rail Road, leased the whole San Carlos Reservation. When the lease wasn't renewed, the cattle were rounded up and moved off. John purchased all the strays from the Aztec and started his own company, the Circle 7, on leased reservation land. His ranch house was in Seven-Mile Wash, and he had a cabin between Pigeon Springs and Hilltop. Then in 1907, John's brother, Earl, rode into San Carlos on horseback looking for him. But when Earl discovered John was up at Fort Apache, a four-day trip by horse, he decided to stay in San Carlos. When he opened a trading post, he became the first trader in the Osborn family."

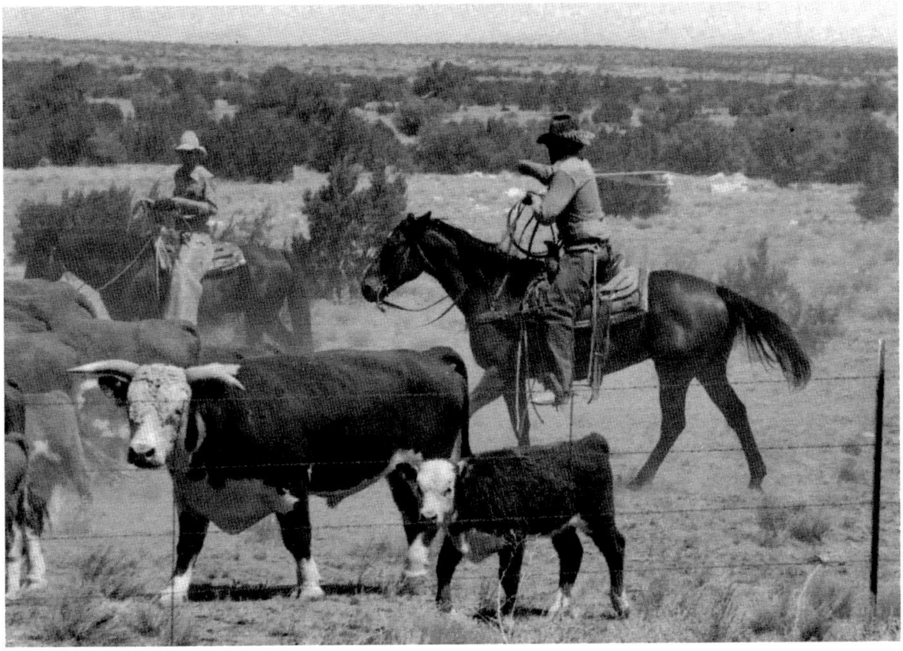

Above: Apache cowboys herd cattle on the San Carlos Reservation, at the time Arizona's largest cattle ranch.

Right: Melvin and Joyce Montgomery, owners of the Peridot Trading Post.

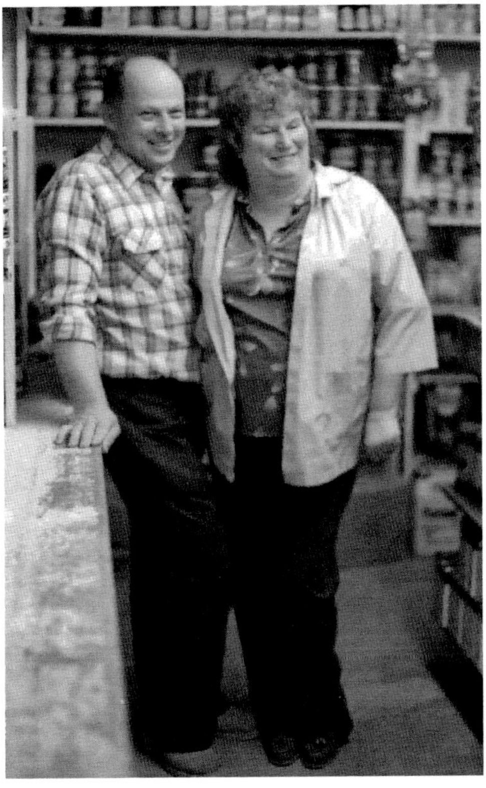

Joyce takes a big breath and settles back against the old wooden display case full of the Apache beadwork that has been traded in for store credit.

"So how did you and Melvin become traders?" I ask.

"I'm getting to that," Joyce says. "Give me a minute." She turns to speak to her butcher, a stocky Apache who is chopping U.S. Prime beef into steaks on an ancient, concave butcher block.

While they confer, I look around the trading post, which is crammed top to bottom with merchandise. Burden baskets of woven cotton willow hang from the ceiling. Dangling from their rims are long ribbons of narrow buckskin, the ends of which are decorated with tiny cones of tin stripped from Crisco cans. The tin cones tinkle in the breeze from the swamp cooler. Beneath the baskets, bolts of red, yellow, green and blue calico line one wall, and cans of peas, corn, beans and Spam the other. Pots, pans, dishware, hammers, nails and wrenches occupy more shelves, and in the center of this cornucopia stands a big old-fashioned soda pop cooler in which Cokes and Orange Crush, root beer and grape drinks nestle in mounds of crushed ice. I love to come to Peridot Trading Post. Sometimes I buy Indian crafts, but mostly I like to visit Joyce Montgomery and listen to her stories.

"In the 1920s," she resumes, "there was, at Old San Carlos, an Apache named Oscar Belvado who grew orchards and sold fruits and vegetables. When the dam was built and the lake covered the town and the orchards, Oscar moved to Peridot and built the original Peridot Trading Company. That was in the '30s. Later, Oscar sold out to Dutch Rupkey—which is why you still hear some people refer to this place as 'Rupkeys'—"

"I thought it was Rukkeys," I interrupt. "I didn't know the name had a 'p' in it."

She laughs. "That's right, *Rukkeys*! That's what people still say. Well, anyway, Dutch, in turn, sold out to my cousin, Earl Dean Osborn, in 1948. Then, in 1951, my father, Harvey Osborn, bought Peridot from Earl Dean and ran it until his death in 1967. The following year, Melvin and I became partners in the family business, along with my mother, Joyce White Osborn."

"Tell about your dad, Joyce Ann," Melvin Montgomery says from behind an enormous antique roll-top desk cluttered with papers and more Apache beadwork.

"You tell," Joyce says, fanning herself with an envelope. "I'm running out of breath."

"Well, old Harvey Osborn was an attorney from Wichita who was just crazy for anybody to talk to," Melvin says. "And years ago there were just dirt roads around here and hardly any salesmen ever made it out this far."

"We were lucky when they did," Joyce says.

"I remember when Joyce Ann and I were first married," Melvin continues. "Whenever somebody from off the reservation came in the store, it was my job to run out back and get Harvey, because he loved to talk. He would talk an arm and a leg off that visitor until the poor guy thought he never would get away."

"So there've been Osborn traders in San Carlos since the early part of the century," I say, marveling at this adventuresome Kansas family who'd become white traders and sunk their roots deep into Arizona soil.

"Yes, but I'm afraid not for much longer," Joyce says. Her normally jolly voice suddenly turns melancholy.

"Why?" I ask, alarmed.

"I can see the handwriting on the wall," she says.

"It's only a matter of time," Melvin agrees. "The Navajo Tribe, for example, has already told their white traders they won't sign any more leases. They're now sending young Navajos to a special training center where they learn how to be traders."

"We're due to sign a new five-year lease, with options to sign for another twenty years," Joyce says.

"But frankly," Melvin adds, "I can't see us staying that long—and I can't see us finding a prospective buyer. Eventually we'll have to do what other traders have done and just sell out our stock. We'll take a loss."

"If we can just hang on 'til the girls get out of college," Joyce says, looking at her husband.

He nods. "The day of the white trader is almost gone," he says as he turns back to his accounts.

Mary Ann

"I think I'll call you Charlie," Chris says to the kitten he finds huddled on our doorstep trying to get out of the rain. A cat? We'd always had dogs. The last cat we owned was the black three-legged one we'd found in the front yard of that terrible house in Shiprock. He really had four legs, but one of his hind legs had been so badly broken that it was twisted completely around. He dragged it after him. We adopted him and gave him the Navajo name of Thomas Yazzie. In spite of his handicap, he was a rather daring cat. He would pick up lighted cigarette butts in his mouth and hobble around the

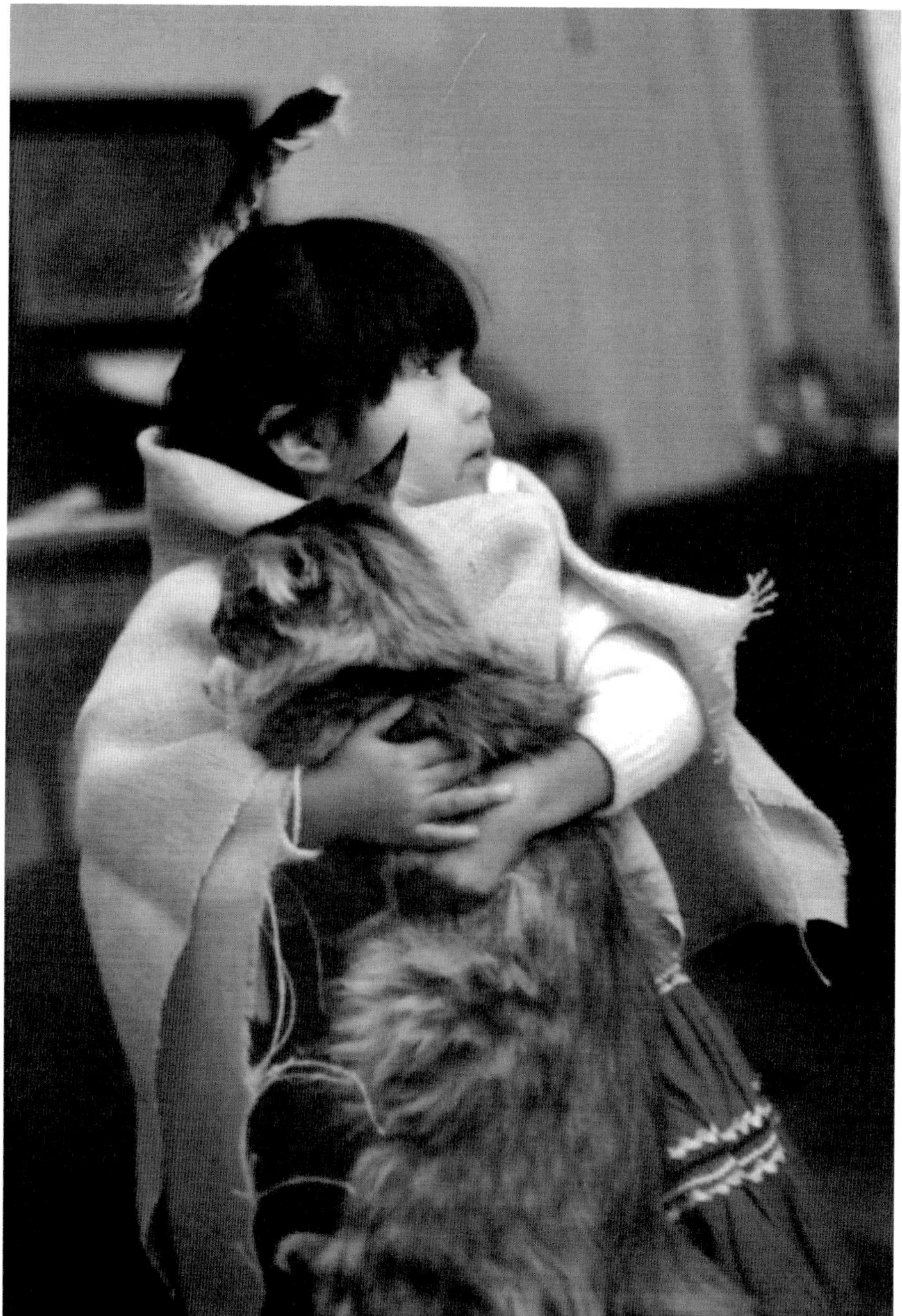

Christy Foxx holds Christopher's cat, Mary Ann.

front yard at night. It was so dark that the only thing you could see was that tiny bobbing spark of light. He died of bubonic plague.

"You'll have to keep Charlie in the garage, Chris,"

"OK, Mom." Chris buries his face in wet fur. After he dries the cat off with a bath towel, we can see it's a longhaired Tabby, mostly gray, with faint stripes of black and yellow. "He's beautiful," Chris says. A few months later, Charlie delivers a litter of four kittens. Two of them die, but a tiger and a pure white one survive.

"I think Mary Ann's a good name for a cat," Chris tells Charlie as he hovers over her cardboard box in the garage. "Mary Ann, my Apache cat." Unlike some cats, Mary Ann proves to be a natural mother. She spends most of her time nursing and bathing her kittens, leaving them only for a few minutes to go outside and scratch in the sand.

"Poor little thing," says my mother who's visiting us. "She hasn't had time to be a kitten herself!"

But Chris takes care of his cat. He delivers her food every day, just as if she's in a hospital maternity ward. He watches carefully while she eats. And then he cradles her carefully, gently, as he will do for the next eighteen years.

Names

I am fascinated with the Apache way of naming things. The Apaches call Globe, the mining town that borders the reservation, *Besh bagowa*. *Besh* means iron, but whether iron refers to the mine or to the bars in the city jail, I have never been able to find out. It seems that iron could refer to either, both the mine and the jail having figured ominously in the lives of the Apaches since the coming of the white man.

The San Carlos Reservation contains two main centers of population: San Carlos, where the tribal government is, and Bylas. San Carlos includes Seven-Mile Wash to the north, Gilson Wash to the south and, between Gilson Wash and Route 70, the little area called Peridot where much of the ground is sprinkled with the rough, green August birthstone. The citizens of Bylas, twenty-five miles to the east, refer to themselves as inhabitants of God's Country and to their cemetery as either Standing By or Ready to Go.

A cluster of federally funded, pastel cinder block houses built during Lyndon Johnson's administration is called Tarzan Valley because of one particular homeowner who occasionally gets drunk, throws open his back door, beats his fists against his chest and yells like Johnny Weismuller in a Tarzan movie from the '40s.

Chinatown, a small group of houses near the Peridot Trading Post, takes its name from a green, wooden two-story structure with a slightly turned-up roof that faintly resembles a pagoda. Newer housing developments are called Taco City (some of the houses have arched windows that look like folded tortillas), Moonbase (the barren mesa suggests the NASA photographs of the Apollo landing) and Hallelujah Square, which is adjacent to a Pentecostal church.

A bridge in Peridot that was covered with water and became impassable years ago during a monsoon rain was named, after the waters receded, Again Bridge.

And for reasons that I cannot fathom, the jail is called New Jerusalem.

Two Girls

Two fourteen-year-old girls begin to visit us after school to play with Noelle. Sarah and Mary are cousins. They both have long, thick black hair, but that is where the similarity ends. Sarah is overweight and has buckteeth. Mary is a classic beauty with her slim figure, high cheekbones and perfect teeth. That Sarah and Mary seem unconcerned by the contrast they make is, to me, striking. Sarah does not orbit around Mary. On the contrary, Sarah is far more gregarious than her pretty cousin.

"White people look so pale," Sarah says to me. Mary giggles. "You and Nellie should go out in the sun," Sarah continues. "Then you would look more interesting."

"We burn," I say, sighing. Mary gives me a cool smile.

One terrible evening, Sarah and Mary stand next to a casket in their grandparents' house. The casket contains the shattered body of their young uncle who blew his head off in that very room. I heard he waved the pistol in the air, threatening his suicide, while Sarah and Mary, alone with him, watched in terror.

As Father Bart begins the third decade of the rosary, I observe the ancient faces of the two young girls. It occurs to me I will never be as old as they are, even if I live one hundred years.

Following the funeral Mass in the Catholic mission, Richard and I stand by the grave at the cemetery on the hill. Father Bart blesses the tortured young uncle one last time, and then he steps back and the medicine man takes his place. As the medicine man begins to chant, I ask Richard's assistant, Joanne Thompson, what he sings.

"He says 'Go away now,' to the dead man's ghost. 'Go away now to where you are supposed to be. Leave us in peace, and don't come back to bother us anymore.'"

After the casket is lowered and the grave filled in with earth, everyone takes a rock to put at the base of the mound. Soon the mound is nearly surrounded with rocks, and as Sarah and Mary add the final stones to complete the circle, I hope for the sake of the two girls and their uncle that the medicine man's prayer works.

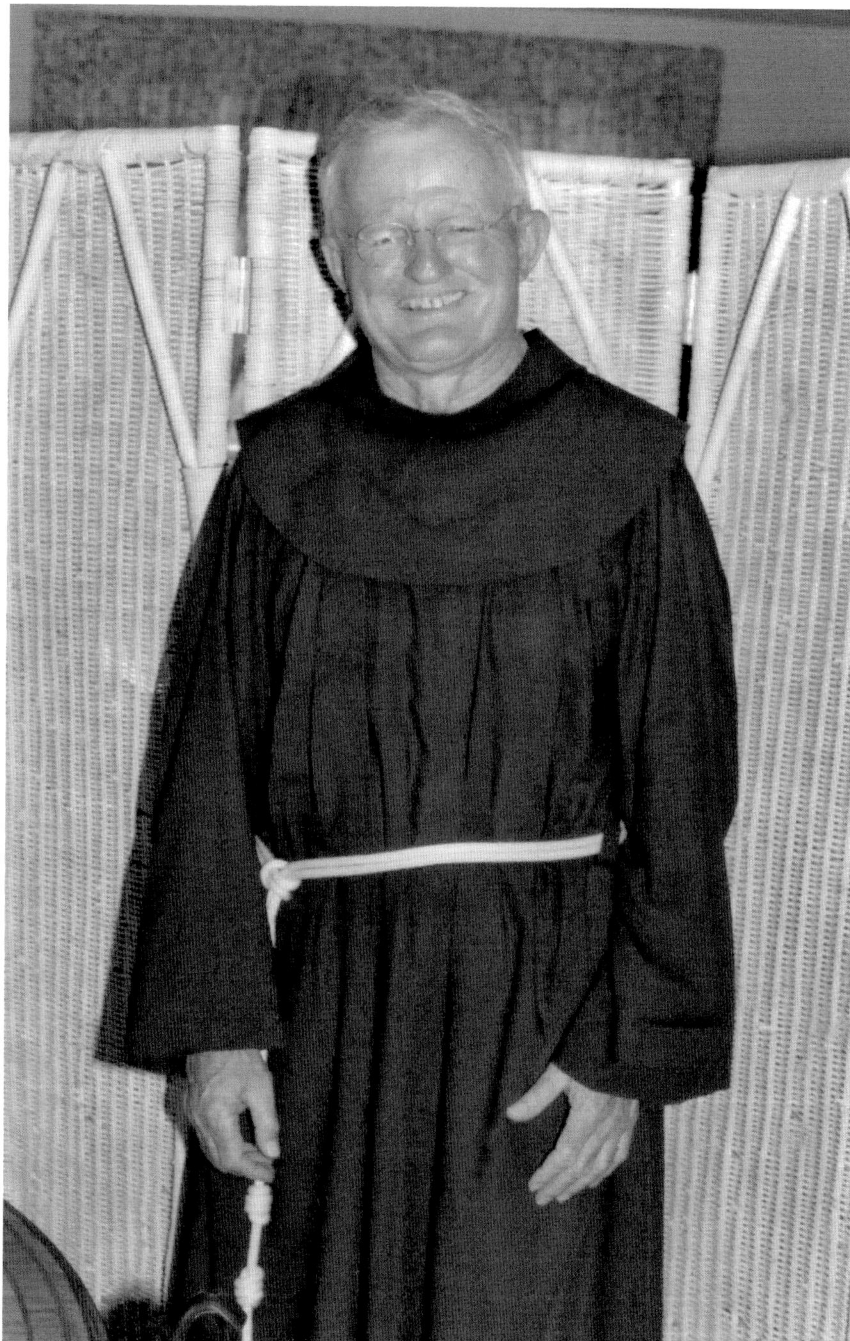

Father Bartholomew, Order of Friars Minor, was made a member of the San Carlos Apache Tribe.

El Santo

The first time I saw Father Bart, I thought he was a brother. It never occurred to me he was the priest in charge of the mission. He was wearing the Franciscan habit, but then in the Order of Friars Minor, priests and brothers dress the same way. He stood at the back door of the convent repairing a broken screen, and as I crossed the lawn toward the school to enroll Patrick in first grade, he stopped hammering, wiped the sweat from his sunburned face and smiled.

He must be the handyman around here, I thought. *The one who's good at fixing things*.

I was certainly right about that. One of the first things I heard about Father Bart when we came to San Carlos was how he had organized the community to pray to end a drought. Not only did he cooperate with the Apache medicine men and enlist the other churches in his successful campaign, but he also managed, somehow, to bring down some Hopi Indians from the reservation up north to do a rain dance. He was already a legend by the time I met him. Father Bart was a member of the Santa Barbara Province, an area covering California, Oregon, Washington, New Mexico and Arizona. The province took its name from one of the most beautiful of all the missions, Santa Barbara on the California coast. The friars of the Santa Barbara Province called Father Bart "El Santo." But even though they called him that in jest, they were absolutely right: he was a saint.

He was the only person in my life with whom I formed an instant friendship. He made it so easy. Bartholomew, one of the twelve apostles mentioned in

Matthew, Mark and Luke, is thought, by many biblical scholars, to be the one called Nathanael in the Gospel of John. It was Nathanael of whom Jesus said, "There is an Israelite who deserves the name, incapable of deceit." That was Father Bart: he possessed a transparent soul and an open heart. And of course he was rich in good works. For example, he operated a one-man sandwich line. But unlike sandwich lines or soup kitchens in urban parishes that functioned at fixed, convenient hours, his was a movable feast that invariably occurred between the hours of midnight and four o'clock in the morning. I doubt if he had slept through the night in twenty years.

Father Bart came out at twelve-thirty one morning to give Richard holy unction when Richard got bean poisoning and our friend Dr. Joe Kryc at the Indian Health Hospital was convinced he was having a heart attack. Father Bart arrived just as we were leaving in the old panel truck that served as an ambulance to go to the hospital in Globe. He would be out for hours on behalf of our family that night, driving up and down the streets and alleys of San Carlos in his brown 1945 Chevrolet pickup truck. My mother, Patti, had phoned him a little after midnight. She'd been awakened by my banging around in my effort to get Richard off the bathroom floor and into the VW bus. By the time Mother threw on her house robe and opened the front door to look outside, she saw only the taillights of our van disappearing around the street corner. As she stood peering into the dark, Joshua, our Saint Bernard, charged her from behind and knocked her down. Thinking of Joshua's pedigree (and how horrified she'd been when she'd discovered how much we'd paid for him), she grabbed onto his tail and clung tenaciously as he dragged her across the front yard. She tried to hold on as he charged over the fence, but when she crashed, face first, into the wooden split rails, her resolution crumbled. Stumbling back to the house, she called Father Bart—not to get help for her own bleeding wounds but to request his assistance in finding the dog, which of course he did. He also took Mother to the Indian Health Hospital, where she was treated.

Behind the mission, in a small area enclosed with a chain-link fence, Father Bart kept his tools, a wheelbarrow, all of his gardening equipment, some old desks from the school, an old claw foot bathtub and one of the pews from the mission. The ten-foot-long pew, with its simple lines, was made from pine, two inches thick, and on the back someone had carved the letters L.A.C. and the date May 18, 1944. Whether that was graffiti or the initials of the carpenter and the year the pew was made I never knew. Father Bart told me he took the pew out of the mission to make room for the baptismal font,

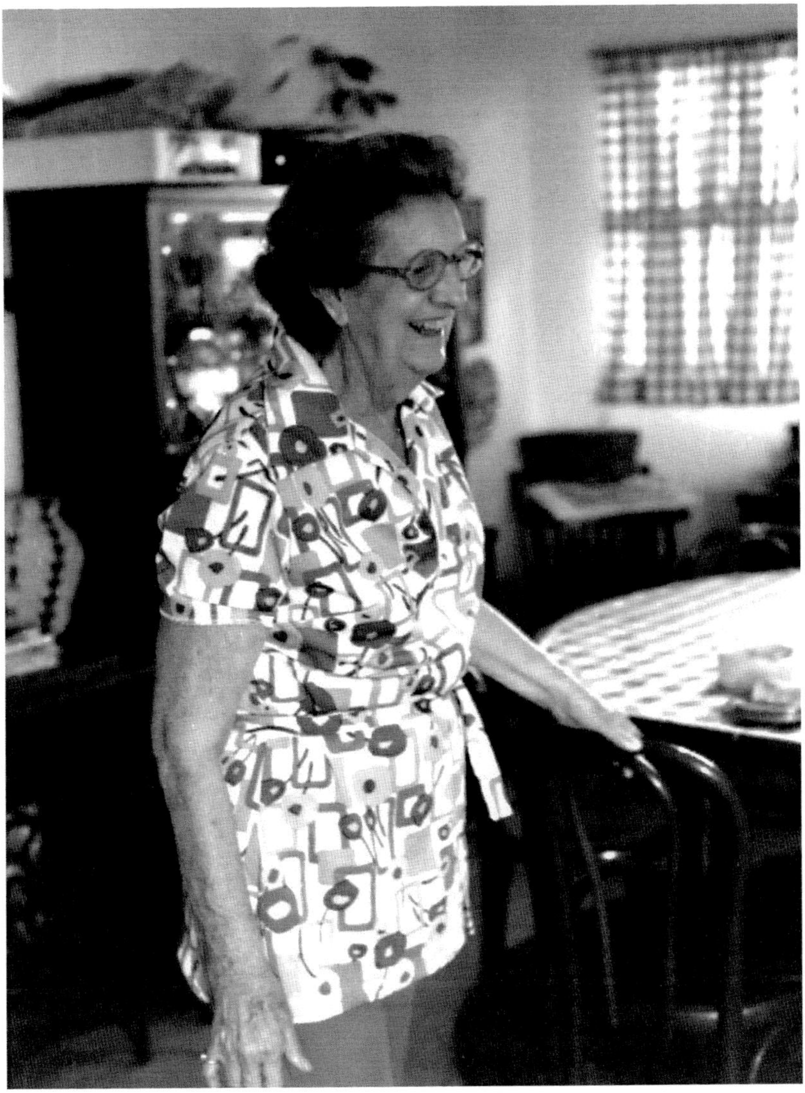

My mother, Patti, called Father Bart to help find Joshua, the Saint Bernard.

when, after Vatican II, baptisms were no longer performed at the entrance of churches but up in front of the congregation. I loved that pew so much that Father Bart gave it to me. One day I looked out the front window of our house and I saw, walking down the street, the two young brothers in their Franciscan habits, Roland in the front and Dennis in the back, carrying the pew on their shoulders.

In the walled yard behind Father Bart's kitchen grew a tall fig tree. Unlike the poor condemned fig tree in Matthew's Gospel, this tree would have delighted Jesus. He would have feasted on that fig tree. It gave a glorious amount of fruit, which Father Bart generously shared with Richard, who, like the Lord, loved figs.

St. Charles School, which Father Bart established with the help of the Sisters of the Blessed Sacrament, provided Apache children (and a few lucky white ones), for a mere five dollars a month, an education worthy of some private institution charging thousands of dollars in tuition.

"In 1958," Father Bart told me, "we made a pilgrimage to help get our school started. St. John's Indian School down near Phoenix loaned us their bus, and we took thirty people."

"Who all went with you on this pilgrimage," I asked him, "and where did you go?"

"Pious Indians from San Carlos and Bylas," he said, his eyes revealing the laughter behind his solemn expression. "We wanted to get Mary's help, so we went down to San Xavier Mission south of Tucson. Have you ever been to San Xavier?"

I told Father Bart that the first pilgrimage I ever made was to San Xavier. I was five years old, and Mother and Daddy and I had been at Aunt Nettie and Uncle Charlie's house in Tucson for Thanksgiving.

"Oh, you must go out to San Xavier Mission," Aunt Nettie had told us. "Everyone goes there. They have this dead saint lying in a glass coffin, and the Indians pin things on his clothes."

My mother's eyes popped at the mention of the dead saint in the glass coffin, but her tourist side won out, and she and Daddy and I drove to the reservation south of town, to the old Franciscan mission, San Xavier del Bac. Years later, I learned San Xavier had been built between 1783 and 1797, under the direction of the Franciscans, by the Tohono O'odham tribe (or Papagos, as they were called then) nearly a century after Father Eusebio Kino, the Italian Jesuit, established a small congregation there.

But it wasn't the reclining statue of St. Francis Xavier covered with Purple Hearts, baby shoes and hospital bracelets that caught my fancy that autumn morning as I walked between Mother and Daddy behind our genial Franciscan guide. Nor was it the frescoed walls crammed with angels in calico skirts, nor the niches filled with exotic saints. I was struck, instead, by the life-sized Mother of Sorrows. I have a full-page photograph of her from a 1950 edition of *Arizona Highways* in which she looks very much as I remember her the first time I saw her. She is dressed in dark blue silk, her hair is covered with a long veil of pale blue satin and she wears a necklace of small metal flowers. Her head is crowned with a heavy halo of enormous golden rays. She clasps her hands together, fingers entwined, over her heart. She has olive skin, high cheekbones and eyes that gaze heavenward.

I stared at her as the guide told us the statue had originally been dressed in real clothes by an eighteenth-century bride whose groom had been killed on the way to the church. The image of the young woman clothing Mary in her own wedding dress was so wonderfully sad.

"But it may be only a legend," the guide said. He told us that the women of the mission dressed the Mother of Sorrows in different clothes for all of her special festivals.

Daddy slipped me a fifty-cent piece to give to the guide.

"God bless you, little one." The Franciscan put his hand on top of my head and smiled down at me. "If it were noon, I'd let you ring the Angelus."

What was an Angelus? I wondered, gazing up at him, wishing I could take his joyous smile home with me, wishing I could take *him* home with me.

"Oh, please can we stay?" I begged.

"That's a whole hour away!" Mother said, laughing along with Daddy and the guide. "We have to get back to Aunt Nettie's for Thanksgiving dinner."

On my knees in the back seat of the car I watched through the rear window as the old white mission with the beautiful lady and the happy Franciscan disappeared behind some ironwood trees and then reappeared once more, but even though I could see it far off, I was afraid I could never find my way back. As the car followed the road over the ridges and down through the washes of the reservation, I thought my heart would break.

"So, that was the first of many visits to San Xavier Mission," I told Father Bart.

"What year did you say that was?" he asked.

"Well, I was five years old, so it must have been 1945."

"I was at San Xavier in 1945," he said.

"Oh, for heaven's sake! And did you..."

"Give the tours? Oh, yes, lots of tours."

"Maybe we met that day!" I said. "Maybe you were the friar who guided us through the mission!"

"*Gah-heh*!" He laughed like an Apache. "Maybe I was!"

Maybe he was. He was the right age. And he had that smile.

Father Bart came to Denver on vacation several times after we left the reservation, and every year, he would stay in our home. "You're my family," he would tell us. We certainly felt that way about him. But the real draw, I

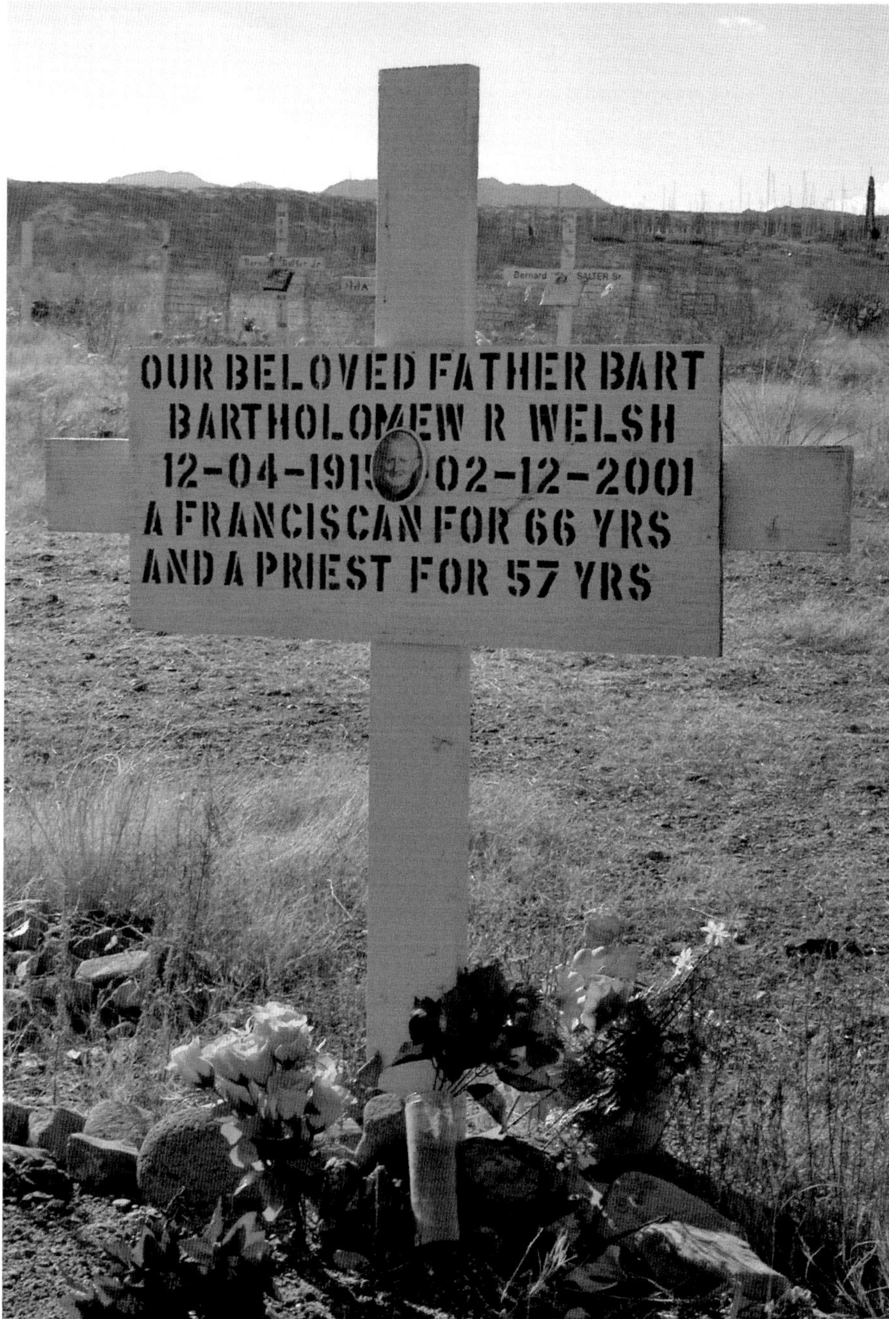

Father Bart's grave in the San Carlos Cemetery overlooks St. Charles Catholic Mission.

know, was Colorado itself. He'd been born in Colorado Springs, and even after serving so many years in the Franciscan missions of California and Arizona, I think he was homesick. One time I found him standing at our big kitchen window, looking down the hill, south, hoping, perhaps, for a glimpse of Pikes Peak.

Years later we would return to San Carlos for the celebration of Father Bart's fiftieth anniversary as a Franciscan. We would hear the tribal chairman read a proclamation making Father Bart a member of the San Carlos Tribe, an honor that has been given, as far as I know, to no other white man. I know he took his membership in the tribe so seriously that when he died in 2001, he was buried, at his request, not in the Franciscan cemetery in Santa Barbara but in the San Carlos Cemetery, on a bluff, facing east, and overlooking the mission he served.

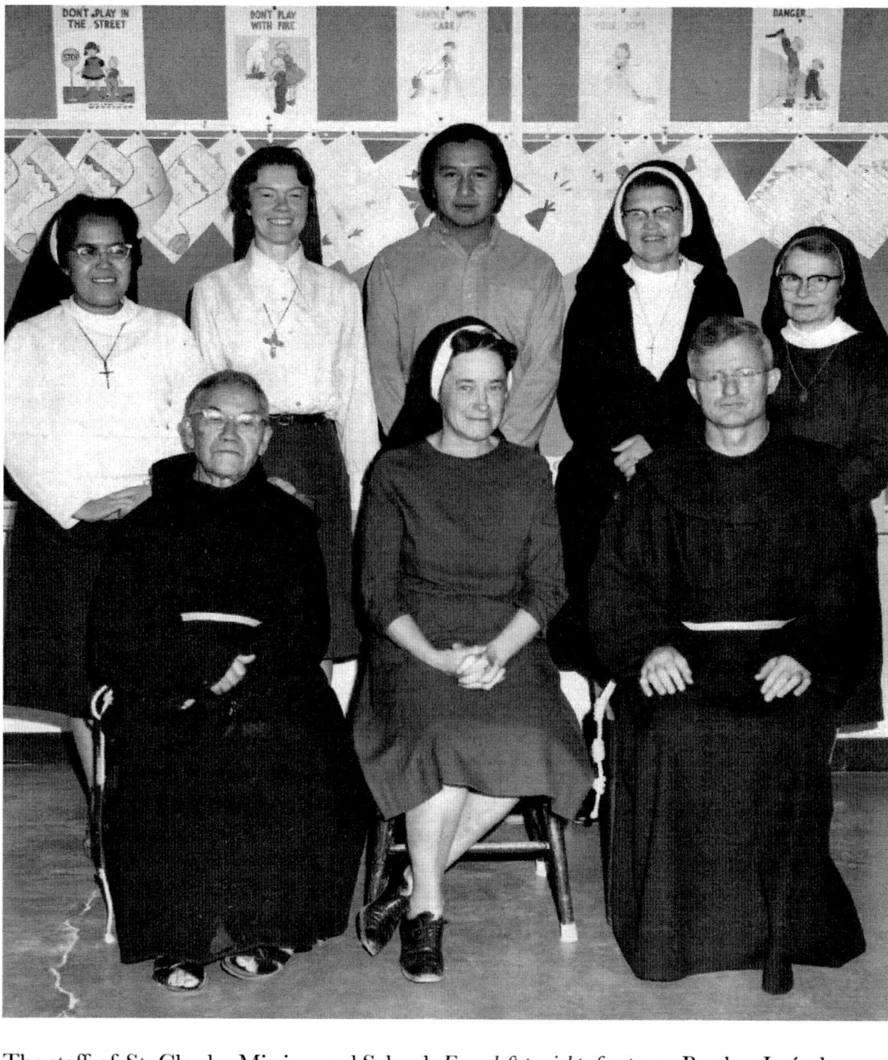

The staff of St. Charles Mission and School. *From left to right, front row*: Brother José; the principal, Sister Anne Regina; Father Bart. *Back row*: Sister Consolata; Sister Mary; the art teacher, Herbert Stevens; Sister Mary Delorey; Sister Patrice. *Photo by the Diocese of Tucson.*

Piñata

Brother José would like a little sherry, if you have some," Father Bart said as he sat in our living room on December 12, 1971, our second Christmas in San Carlos. "A little sherry for Brother, if you please." He sipped his own iced tea. The five nuns (also drinking iced tea) trilled politely as Richard filled a crystal water glass with Dry Sack and handed it to the very old man in the long, brown habit who was bent nearly double in our Lincoln rocking chair.

"Gracias, Ricardo," Brother José said in his high, thin voice. Golden liquid lapped the edges as the old Franciscan lifted the goblet to his lips and swallowed. He sighed with pleasure, settled back as far as his hunched body would allow and looked around the room.

"This is a very special day for Brother José," Father Bart said.

Brother José stared at him with a quizzical expression.

"A very special day for you, the Feast of Guadalupe," Father Bart repeated loudly, looking directly into Brother José's face. Brother José nodded and grinned. "Brother José has a great devotion to Our Lady of Guadalupe," Father Bart continued, nearly shouting, "but he hadn't been able to visit her since he left Mexico during the revolution. I took him back to Mexico City a few years ago, and he danced—you should have seen him!—he *danced* right up the aisle of the shrine!"

The nuns giggled. Noelle, on Sister Anne Regina's lap, laughed, too, wiggling her fingers, which were encased in the tiny white gloves the sisters had brought her for a Christmas present.

"I swear I couldn't keep up with him!" Father Bart finished. "He wore me out!"

"We would always have piñatas," Brother José said, slowly churning out the words. "For nine whole days before the feast. One piñata every day. Like a novena. A piñata novena!"

Surprised by Brother José's rare speech, I looked at his face, childlike in its sudden intensity. A *piñata* novena? How could you have a piñata novena? Wasn't a novena something you prayed?

Sister Consolata grinned at Brother José conspiratorially. "In my pueblo at Laguna we don't have piñatas, but sometimes we dress up like butterflies and buffaloes and dance in the plaza in front of the church."

Butterflies and buffaloes dancing together? Now there was an image!

"But I love piñatas, too," Consolata said.

"I love piñatas," Brother José echoed in his wavery voice.

"We have a piñata!" Christopher, followed by Patrick, suddenly charged through the front door and into the house.

"You do?" Father Bart said.

"We have a piñata and it's full of candy and we get to break it tonight!" Chris shouted, twirling around the room.

Brother José's eyes widened.

"Can we break the piñata now, Dad?" Chris asked.

"We have to wait, Chris," Patrick said. "The piñata's for after dinner. Isn't it, Dad?"

"Why can't we break it *now*?" Chris demanded.

"Sure. Why not?" Richard said, his eyes upon Brother José. "Let's break that piñata right now!"

Brother José handed his empty glass to Father Bart, who helped him up from the rocking chair. He shuffled behind the rest of us to the patio out back where we'd strung up a cheerful-looking orange and yellow lion we'd bought from a street vendor in Nogales, Sonora.

"Can I be first, Dad?" Chris asked. "Please?"

I tied the dish towel around Christopher's eyes, put the stick in his hands and turned him around three times. I yelled as he lunged toward the nuns, barely missing Sister Patrice's face.

"Mind my head, darling boy!" the little Irish nun cried.

Richard quickly yanked Chris back in the direction of the piñata. On Christopher's third and final try, Richard lowered the rope enough so the stick grazed the lion. Disappointed, Chris pulled off the dish towel and blinked at the light.

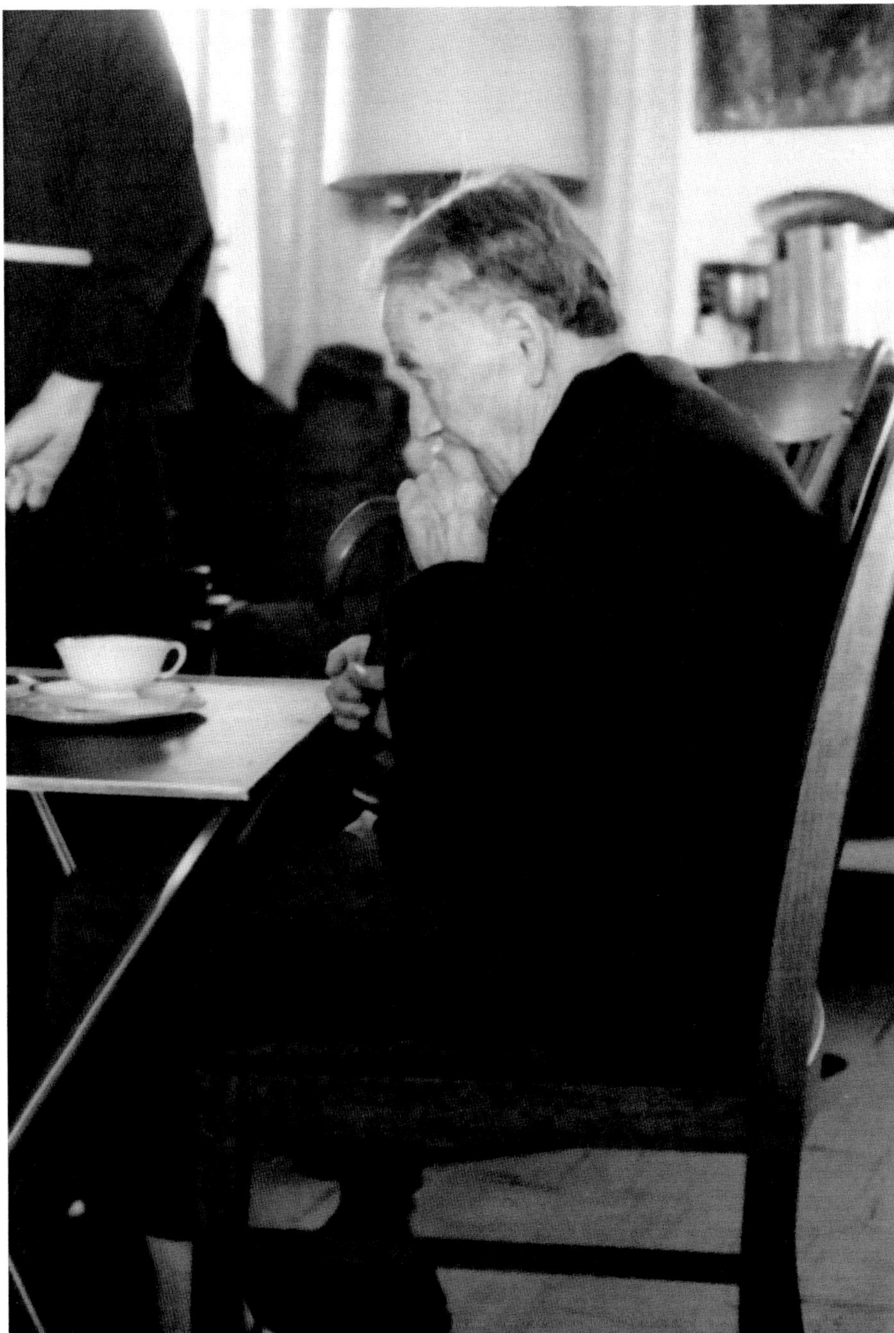

Brother José at the piñata party.

"Don't worry," I consoled him. "If someone else breaks the piñata you'll be able to *see*! That way you can find more candy!"

Patrick swung at the piñata with no more success than Chris, and then, one by one, we all took turns, even Brother José, who tottered back and forth but then surprised us by grazing the lion's side. Finally, Sister Anne Regina struck the lion with such force that he exploded into a shower of candy, scattering licorice, lemon drops and miniature chocolate bars over the patio and out onto the dried grass of the backyard. Wrapped in glittering cellophane, they twinkled, seductive as tiny stars in the yellow light from the porch lamp. Like vultures, we shrieked with laughter and swooped down on the grass, bumping into each other.

And then I saw Brother José resolutely inching his way toward a solitary lemon drop lying at the edge of the patio. The lemon drop, like Brother José, had somehow been overlooked by the rest of us.

Christopher saw it, too. Mortified, I watched my greedy little boy, the pockets of his Levi's already bulging with candy, reach out and grab the lemon drop from beneath Brother José's quivering fingers. I opened my mouth, but before I could speak I saw Chris glance up at Brother José. He stared hard for a few long seconds, a battle clearly raging across his round little face. Suddenly, he handed over the lemon drop.

"Gracias," Brother José whispered.

Christopher hesitated for a moment, and then he dug down into his jeans and brought out a chocolate bar and placed it next to the lemon drop on the palm of Brother José's hand. Delight flashed across Brother José's face, and I watched, astonished, as Chris emptied his pockets and filled up the old man's hands until they overflowed. We followed Brother José as he turned and shuffled back into the house. Perhaps, in his mind, he was back in Mexico seventy years ago, scoring big on the ninth day of his piñata novena.

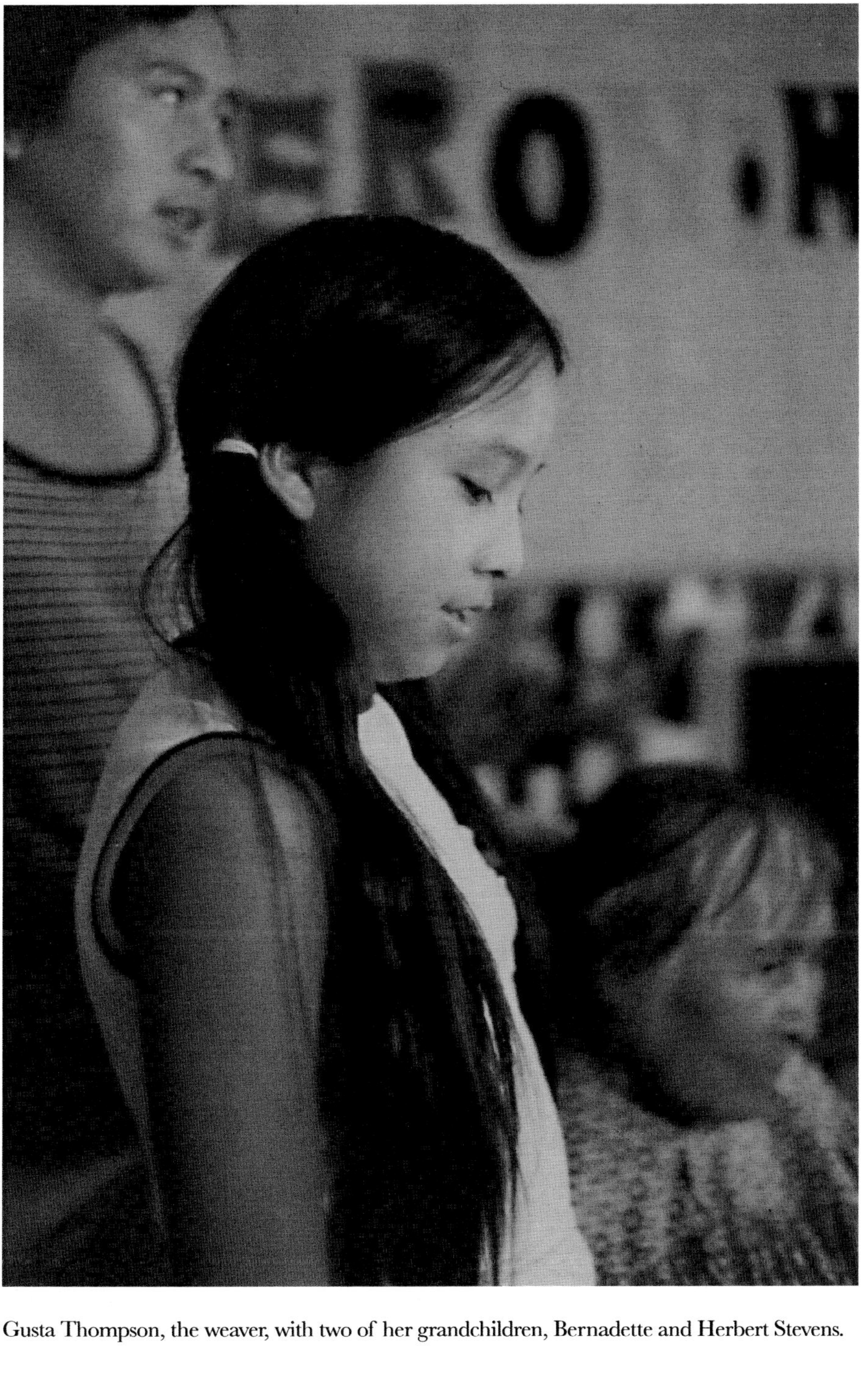

Gusta Thompson, the weaver, with two of her grandchildren, Bernadette and Herbert Stevens.

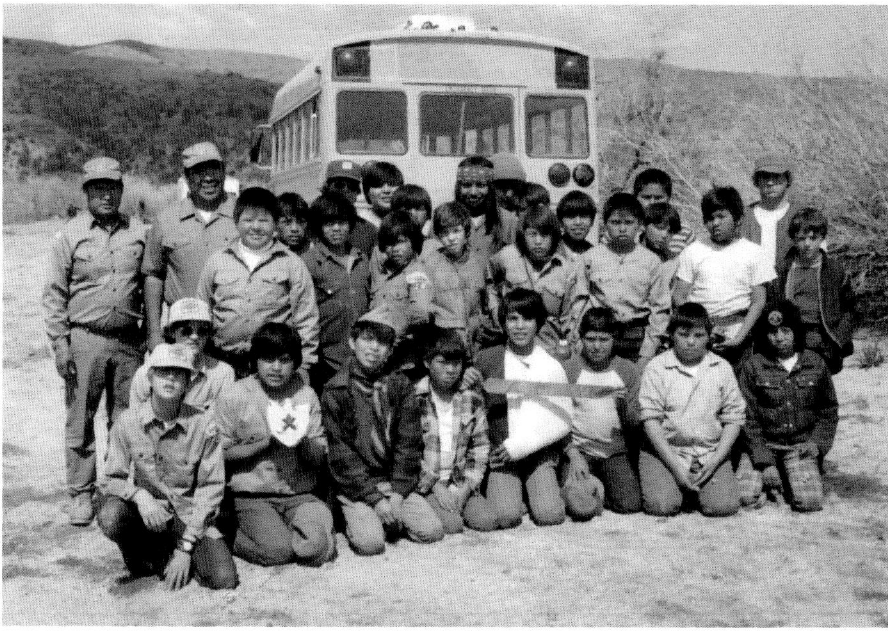

Patrick's Boy Scout troop. Patrick is on the far right in the second row. *Photographer unknown.*

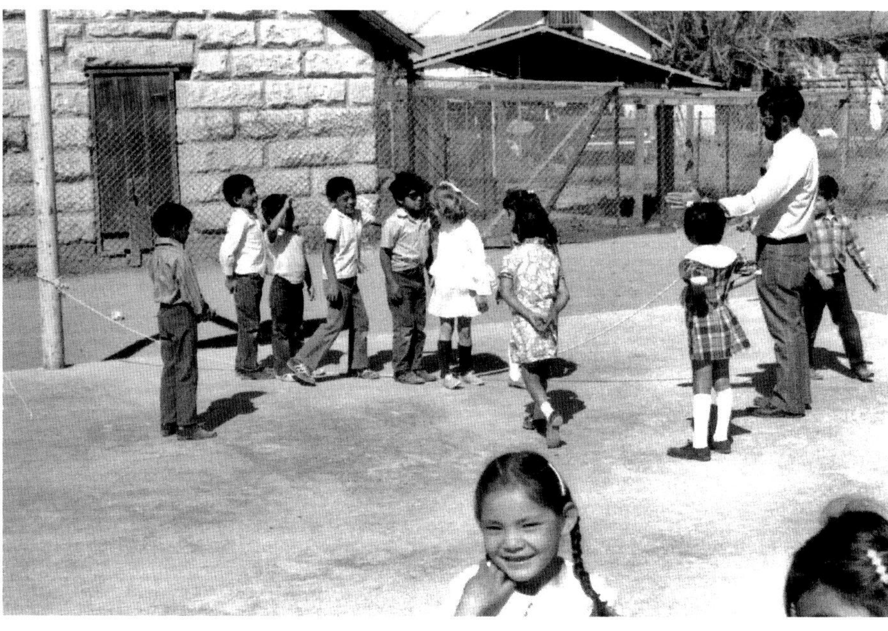

Richard on the playground with students from St. Charles School.

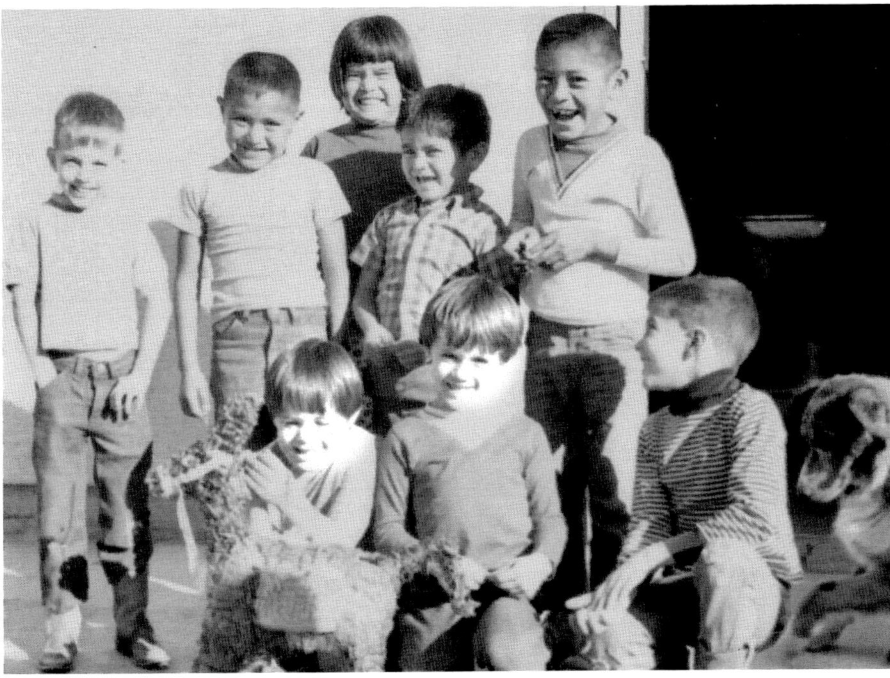

Patrick's seventh birthday party.

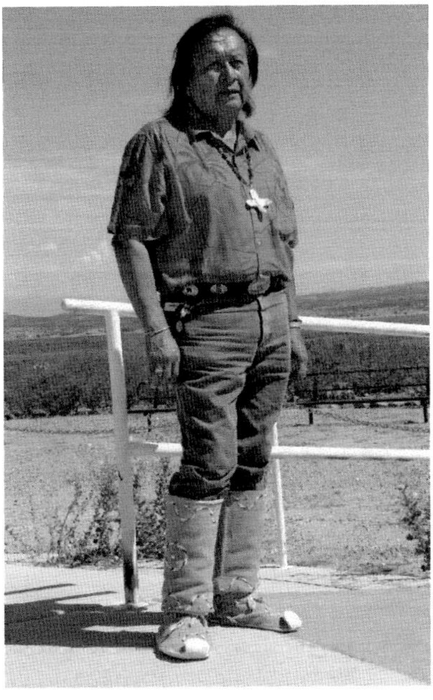

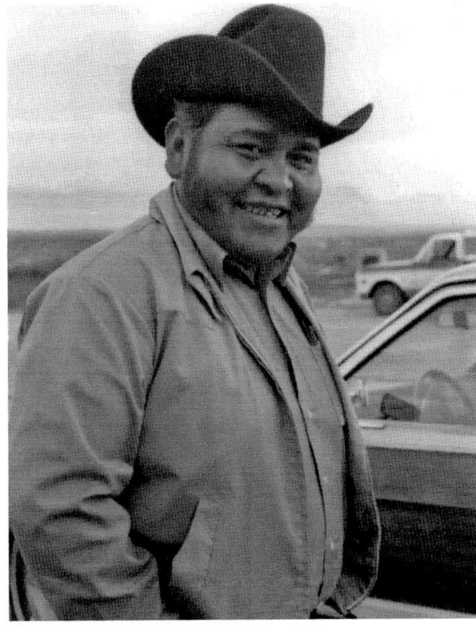

Left: Herb Stevens, director of the San Carlos Cultural Center, 2014. *Right*: Edmund Wesley, son of Clarence Wesley and vice-chairman of the tribal council.

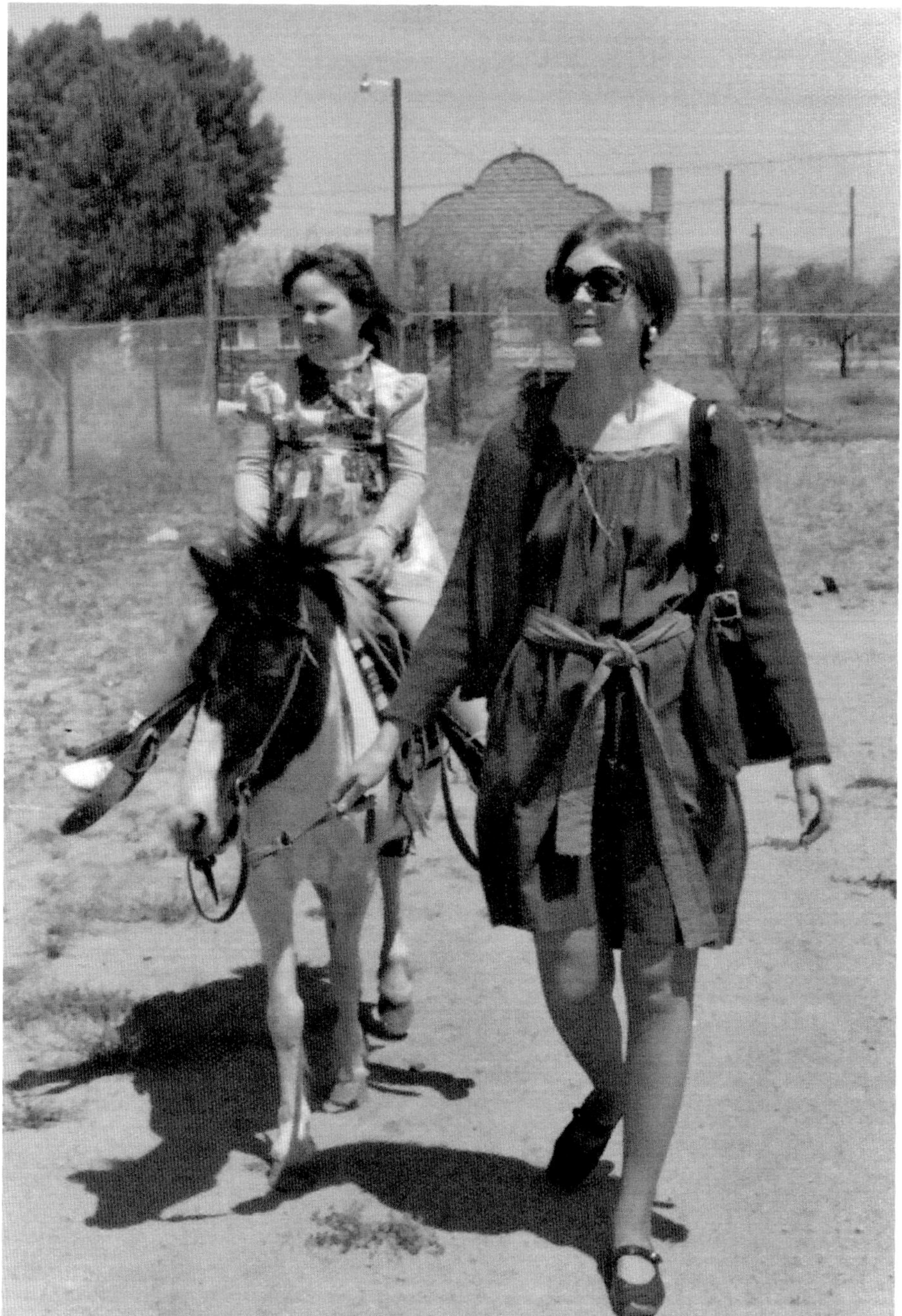

I lead Noelle on a pony at the school fair.

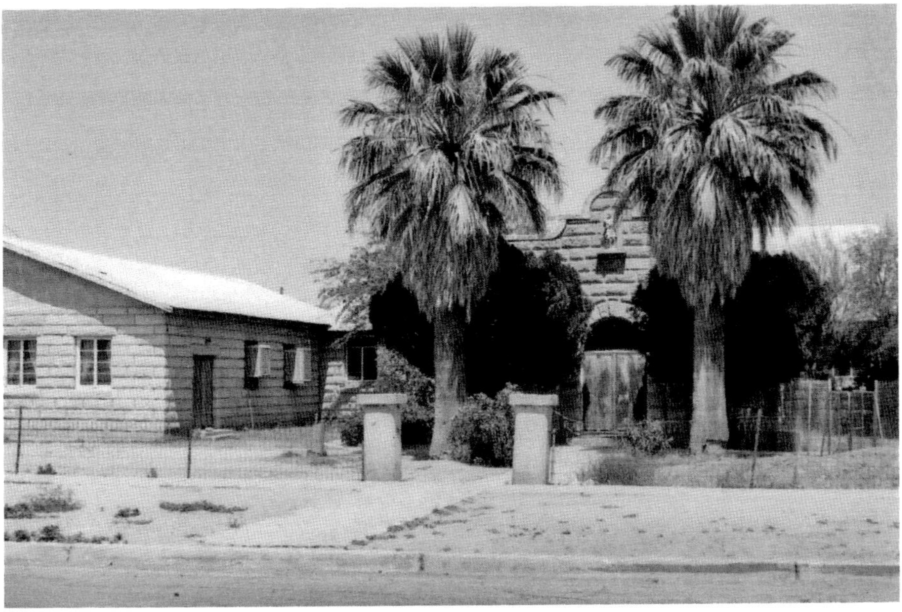

St. Charles Catholic Mission, San Carlos.

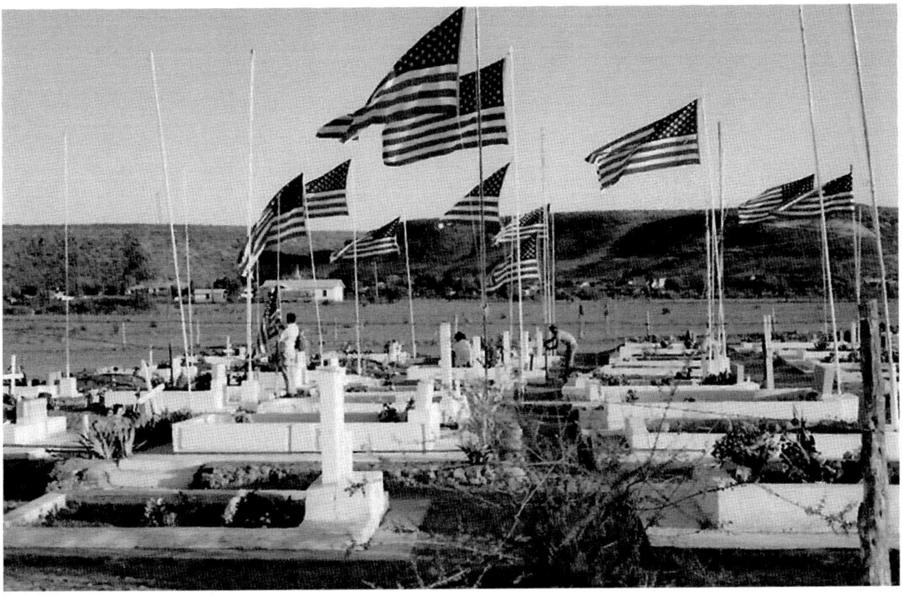

American flags fly over the graves of Apache warriors who fought for the United States.

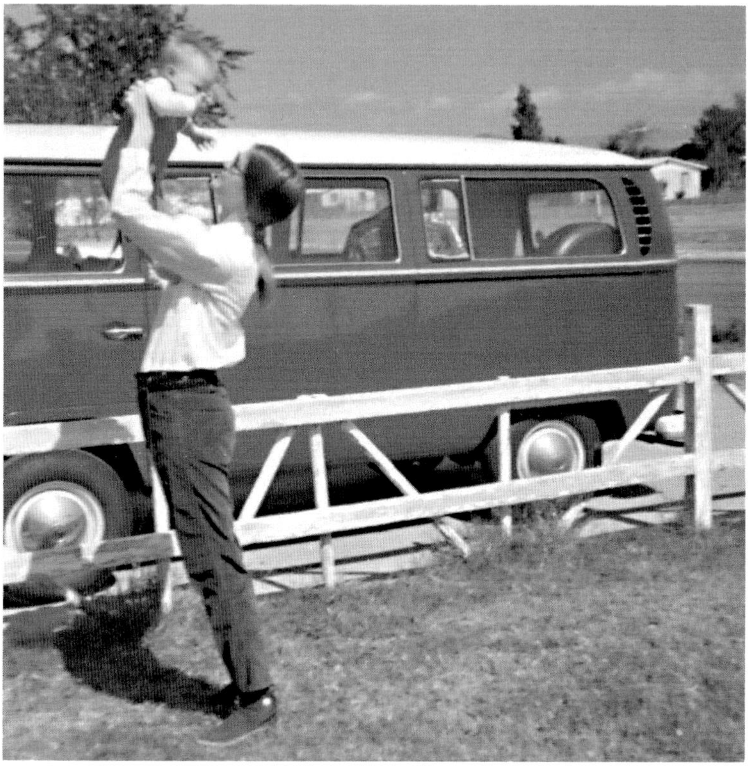

I am holding Noelle next to the red VW bus our first year in San Carlos.

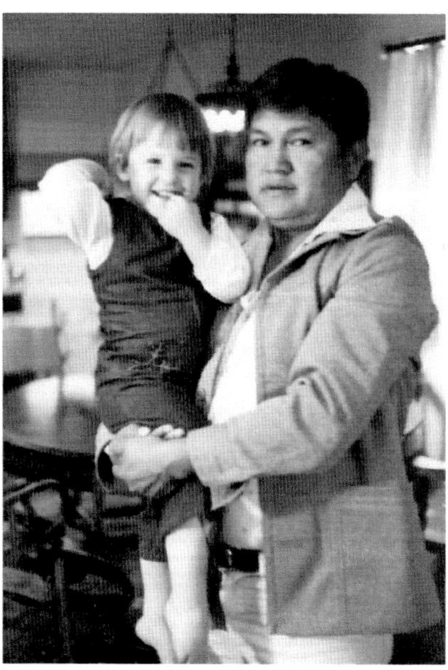

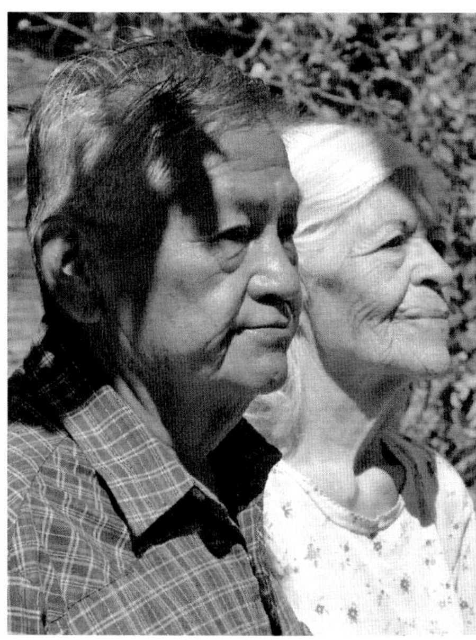

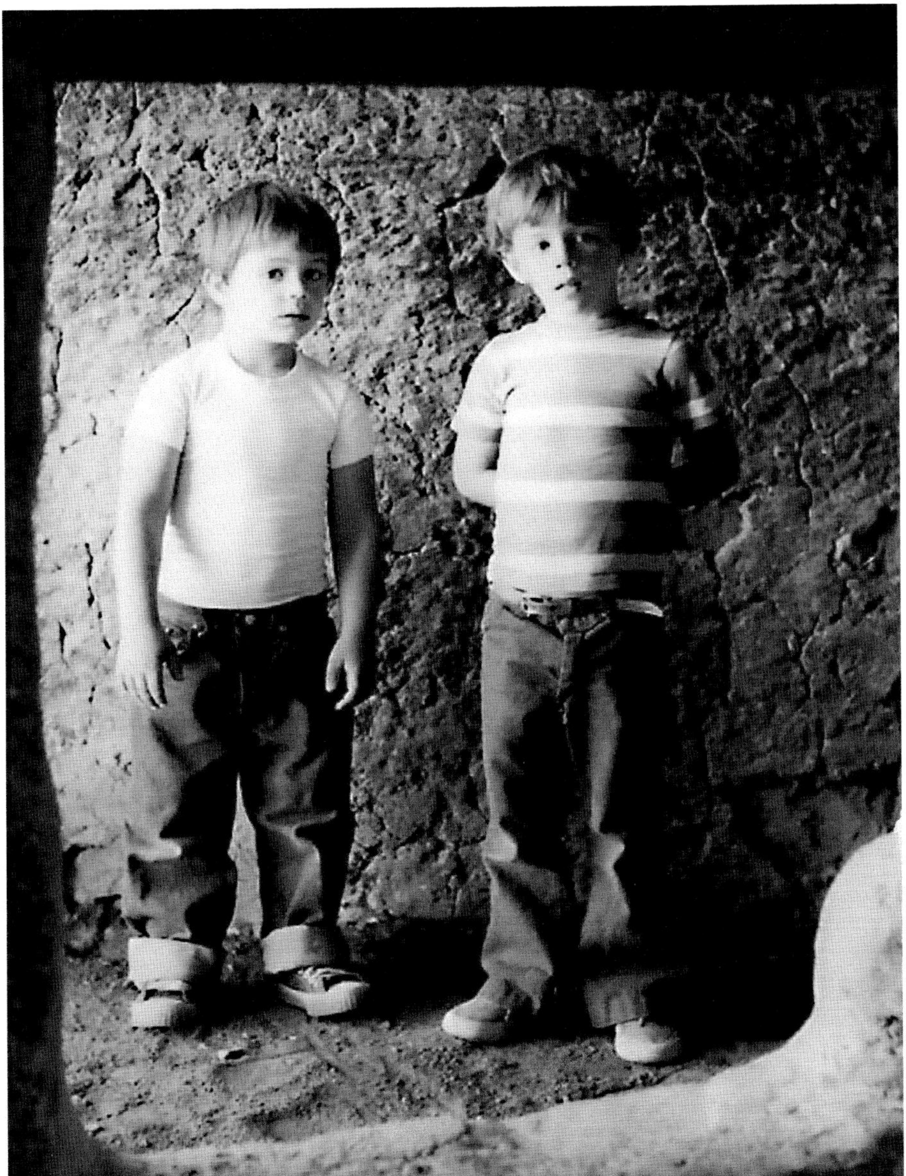

Christopher and Patrick peer into a room of the ancient Salado ruins in Tonto National Forest.

Opposite, bottom left: Our youngest child, Holly, with her Apache godfather, Raleigh.
Opposite, bottom right: Holly's Apache godfather, Raleigh Thompson, and Pima godmother, Joanne Thompson, in 2014.

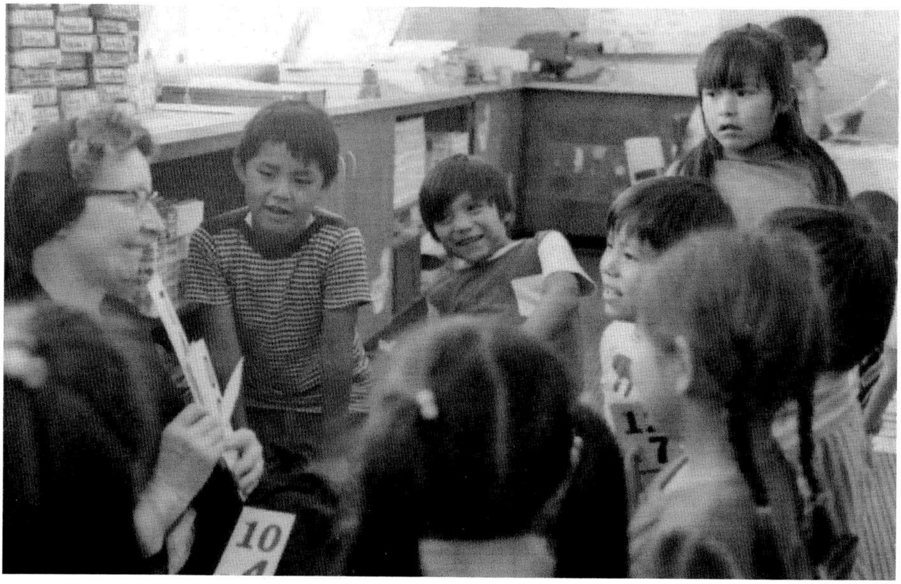

Sister Inez holds class outdoors at St. Charles School.

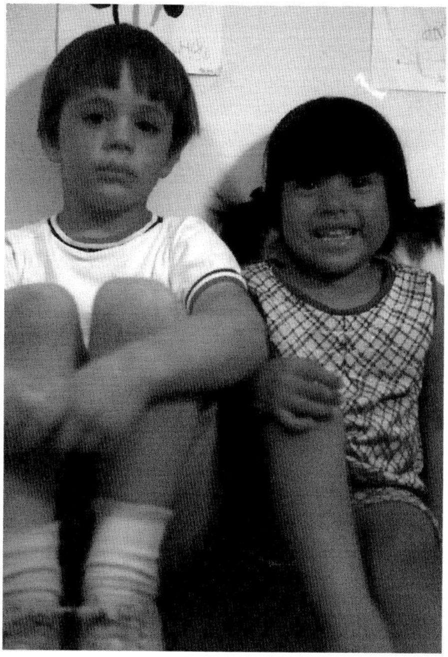

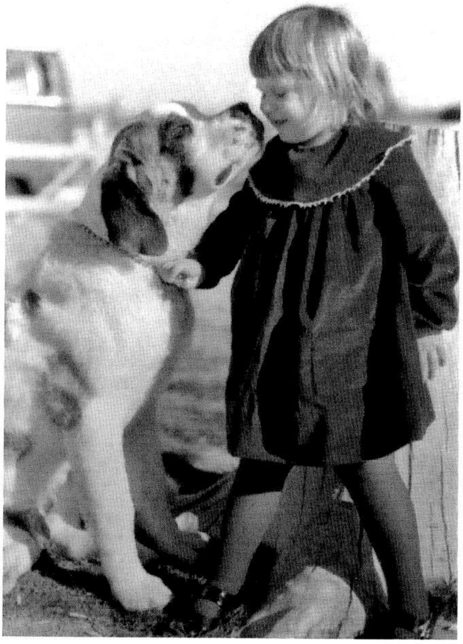

Left: Christopher and his friend Christy Foxx. *Right*: Noelle with Joshua, our Saint Bernard.

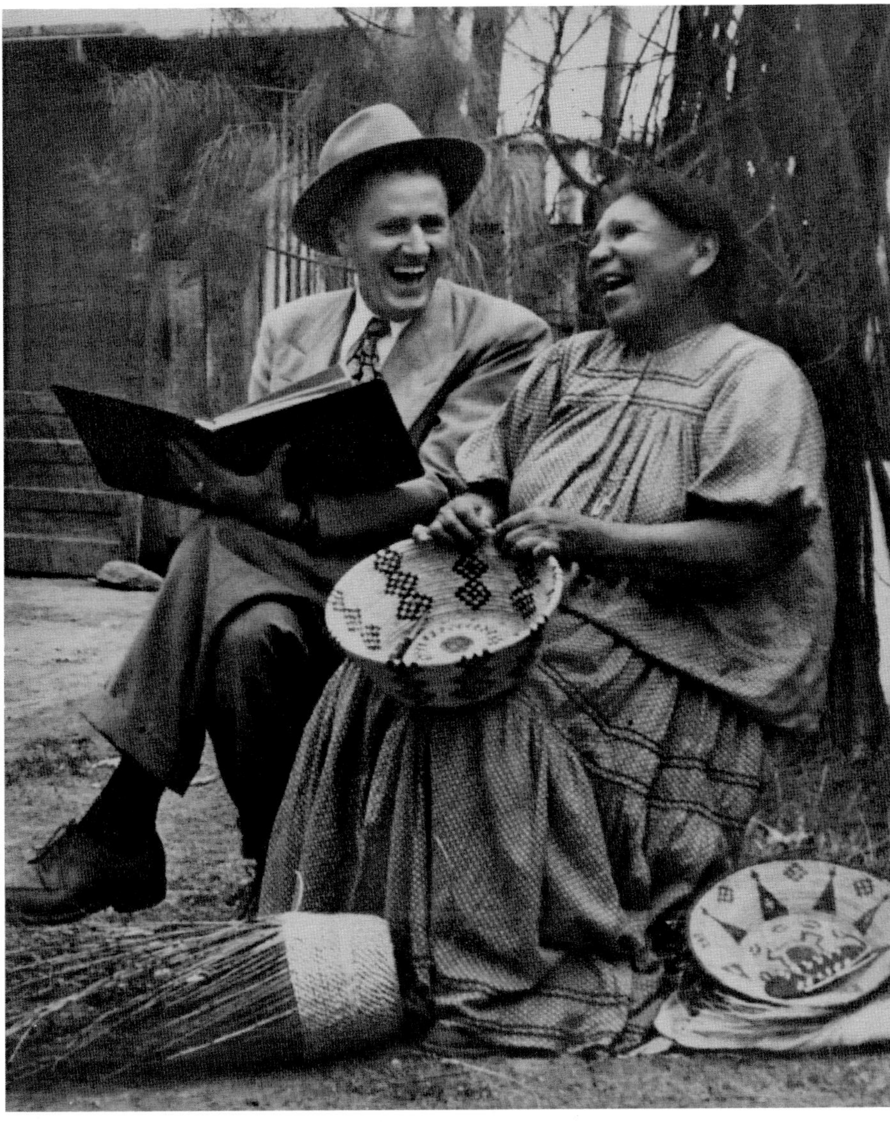

The anthropologist Wayne T. Pratt with the Apache weaver Lizette Phillips. *Photo by Russell Mishler.*

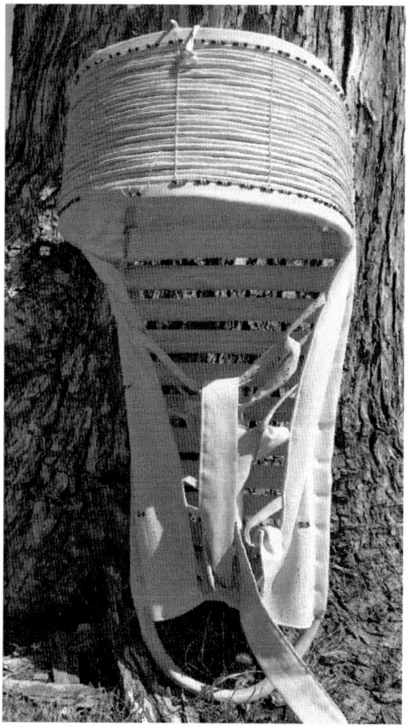

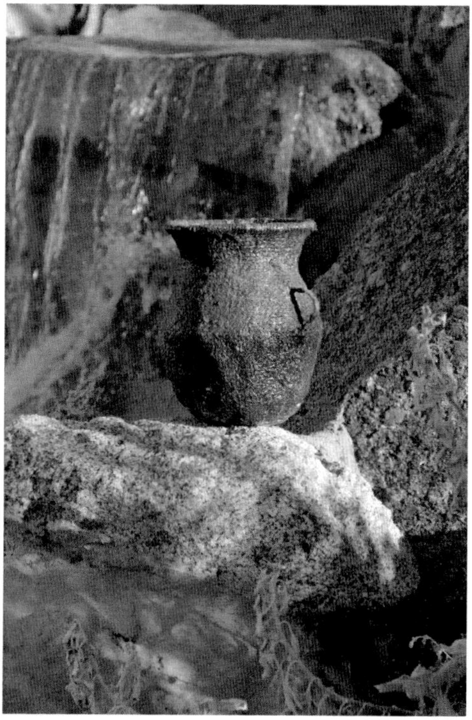

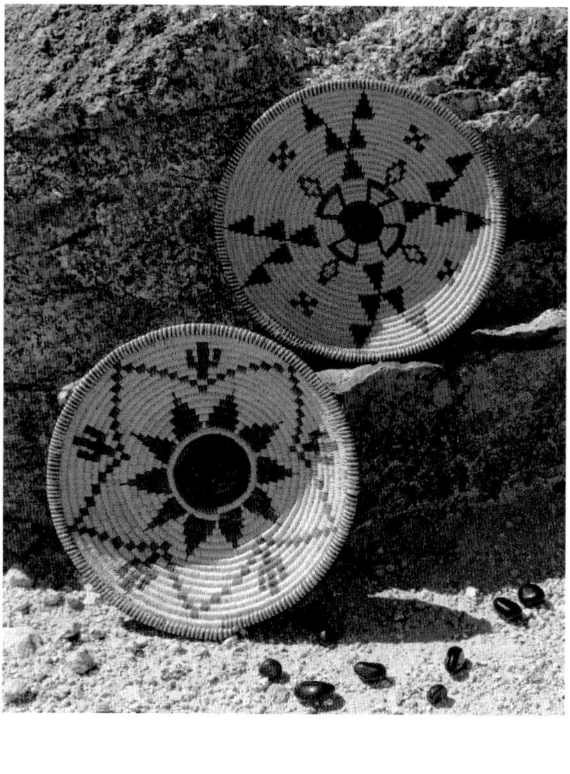

Above, left: Our baby Holly's Apache cradleboard, a gift from the women of St. Charles Catholic Mission.

Above, right: An Apache basket covered with boiled pine pitch is called a *tu's*. It makes a fine water carrier.

Left: The food basket with saguaros was made by Celena Perry; the basket on top was woven by Gusta Thompson.

Opposite, bottom left: An Apache drum from the 1930s is painted with a picture of a Gáán dancer.

Opposite, bottom right: Saguaro-covered mountains where Apaches once roamed freely.

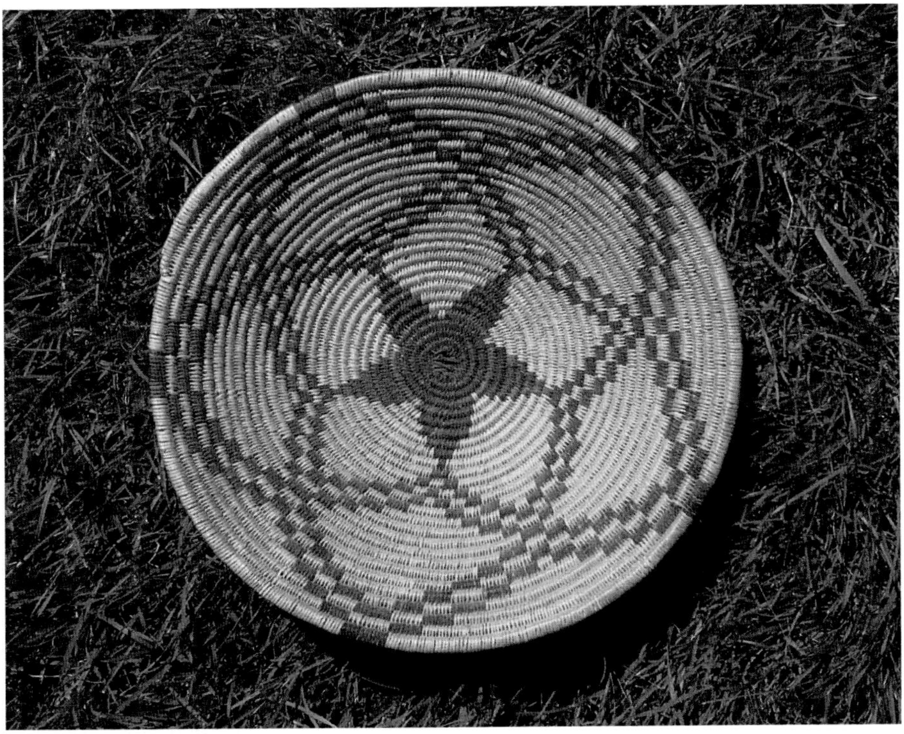

The food basket was woven by Celena Perry.

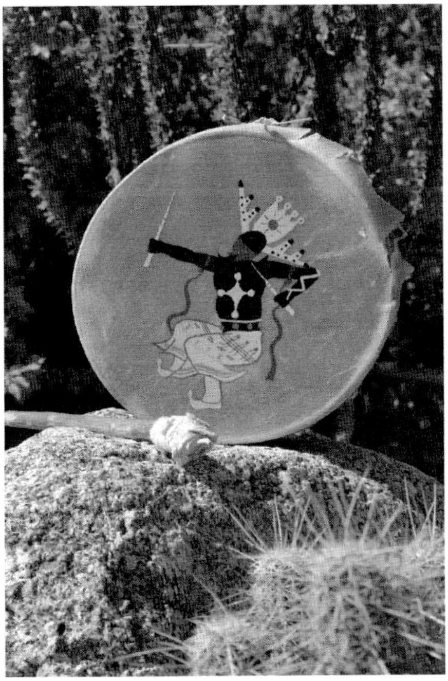

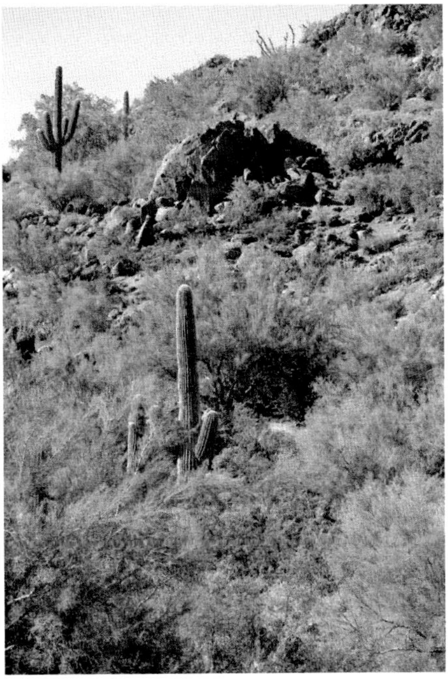

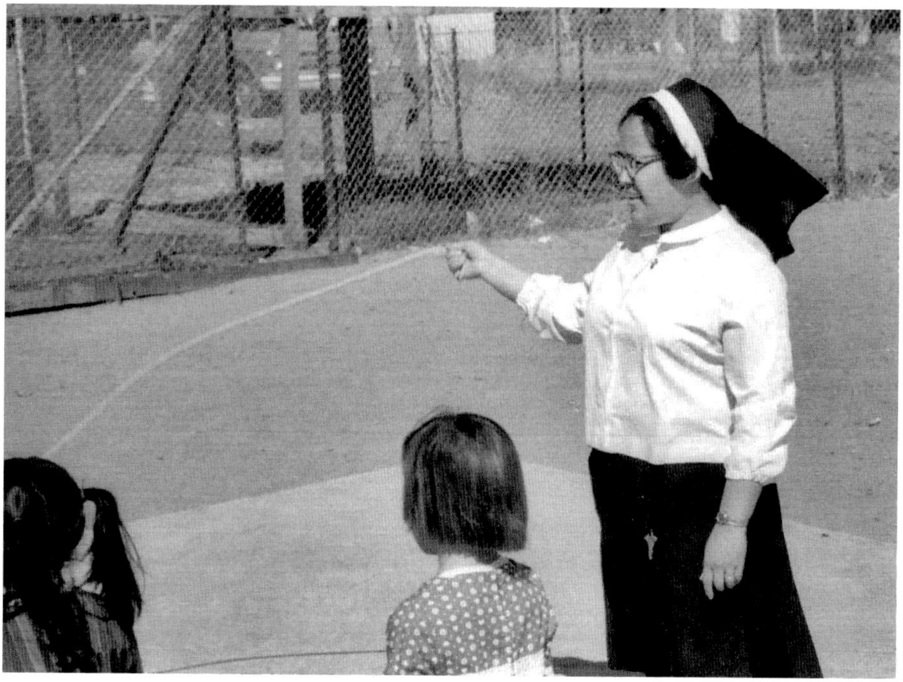

Sister Consolata, from the Laguna Pueblo in New Mexico, is on the playground with her class at St. Charles School.

Consolata

"Why would they trust you?" Sister Consolata said. "You're white."

I knew she was right, but I was stung by her comment. We'd been discussing the Catholic mission youth group Richard and I were tempted to abandon. Occasionally, two or three people drifted in or out of meetings at our house. The whole thing was an embarrassment to us because we weren't sure why the group existed or why we were the sponsors. I think it was an effort to give Richard and me a way to be involved in the mission.

"I don't think they really trust us," I'd said to Sister Consolata, eliciting the response, which, unlike her name, gave me no consolation. Her moods, which shifted between friendly and hostile, threw me off balance. She had been warm and open when I first met her, but she had quickly revealed another aspect of her personality when she took offense at my feeble attempts to become involved in the mission.

"We don't need your big city methods here," she'd once said when Richard and I, in response to her questions about our life in Chicago, told her about some of our experiences in the peace and civil rights movements. What in the world did she think we might do? Demonstrate in front of the church? And for what?

Sister Consolata was from the Laguna Pueblo in New Mexico. The Lagunas, as well as the other dwellers of the ancient pueblos, appeared to consider themselves superior to the "wild" and once nomadic Apaches and Navajos who had been in the Southwest for only a few hundred years. I wondered if Sister Consolata trusted white people. I did not think so. I wondered why she trusted the white man's religion. I couldn't resist asking her. Her round body stiffened, her blue veil fluttered, her eyes glittered behind her glasses.

"My family has been Catholic for almost three hundred years."

I did not contest that. The beautiful church at Laguna had been built in 1699.

I knew, of course, that as the token Native American on the mission staff, Sister Consolata was in a delicate position: did she identify with the Indians whom she taught or with the white mission staff with whom she was officially affiliated? Could she do both? Could she *be* both? As a white woman who had worked in a black civil rights organization, I sympathized. It was easy to feel out of place. Nevertheless, I was tired of her moods.

Sister Consolata disarmed me once again near the end of the school year when she invited Chris to a kindergarten party "to help him get used to the idea of starting school in the fall." I told her Chris would love a party, and I would love a couple of hours of quiet. I thanked her.

"Christopher was perfect today," Sister Consolata told me when I walked to the school to meet Chris after the party.

"He was?" I said, relieved that my rambunctious little boy had behaved well.

"I've discovered a special bond between us," she said. "Lizards."

Lizards?

"I am a member of the Lizard clan in my pueblo," she said.

"You are?"

"It's very hard to catch lizards," Sister Consolata continued. "Do you know how Christopher does it?"

"No." What on earth was she talking about?

"He showed me. He stares at the lizards and they don't move. They let themselves be caught."

She gazed down into Christopher's eyes, which were brown; today, they looked a little green.

"Little Lizard Brother," she said, patting him on the head. He looked up at her in adoration.

To my disappointment (and to Christopher's), Consolata was moved to first grade in the fall, and Chris did not have her when he started kindergarten, nor did he have her in first grade. The two lizards would never spend time together in the classroom. Perhaps she adored him too much, and in a Catholic school, that would, I think, never be allowed.

"They're not allowed," Sister Consolata would tell me a couple of years later. "Particular friendships, they're not allowed in the convent."

"What do you mean by 'particular friendships'?"

"We're not allowed to be close to one person in particular," she said. "We have to be equally friendly with everyone."

"How in the world is that possible?" I asked. "How can you like everyone the same?"

Sister Consolata sighed and looked out the window.

We were returning to the reservation from Phoenix, she and I, after a workshop on church music by the African American priest Father Clarence Rivers, which had been presented at the Franciscan retreat house, Casa de Paz y Bien. Sister Consolata, who was in charge of music for the Sunday service at St. Charles Mission, had invited me to go along with her. The sisters would pay my registration fee. I offered to drive.

The workshop had been terrific. Father Rivers had taught about fifty of us to loosen up, to clap our hands and move around a little. I thought I was back at Operation Breadbasket in Chicago. We sang a lot of songs, but the one everybody seemed to love the most was a real soul-stirrer called "Ride On King Jesus." Back in San Carlos we sang it on Palm Sunday, while the whole congregation, waving big palm branches, walked around and around outside the tiny church. Consolata played her guitar and led the way.

How strange it seems to me now, in looking back, that we never knew ahead of time which sisters would remain with us and which ones would be transferred to a new assignment. They would all leave for their motherhouse in Pennsylvania for the summer; in the fall, some of them would return and some would not. There were no goodbyes.

Consolata told me a story of one of her earlier assignments, which had been in New Orleans at Xavier University, a school established by the Sisters of the Blessed Sacrament for the benefit of African Americans. (Their mission, as stated by their founder, Mother Katherine Drexel, was to African Americans and Native Americans.)

When Consolata was a child, perhaps ten or eleven years old, a group of Mormon missionaries came to Laguna Pueblo. Consolata recalled that the missionaries took a group of children, herself included, to a summer camp where they were baptized into the Mormon Church. It seems a strange thing to have happened to Consolata, considering her family's long history as Roman Catholics. After Consolata returned from the summer camp, she had no further connection with the Mormon Church. She remained a Roman Catholic. One evening in New Orleans, many years later, Consolata was told she had two "gentlemen" visitors. Consolata, accompanied by another sister, went to the parlor where two men introduced themselves as representatives of the local Mormon ward. Her baptismal record in the Mormon Church had been forwarded to them, they had tracked her down and they needed to know her intentions. Would she return to the Mormon Church? If not, they would have to excommunicate her.

Consolata was stunned. "This was before we wore modern habits," she said. "So there I was in my long black dress, my black veil, standing in the parlor of my Catholic convent, and I was going to be excommunicated from the Mormon Church."

I laughed.

"It sounds funny, I know," she said, "but it was also a little scary. Excommunication! They excommunicated me, said all of these terrible words, I can't even remember them all, but they went through me like a knife." She put her hand over her heart. "I just stared at those men. And then they left."

And then they left.

And then Consolata would leave. I knew. I knew that day when, at the end of our third year in San Carlos, I saw her with Sister Anne Regina next to the big old mesquite tree in the grassy courtyard between the school and the convent. Consolata held up a necklace for me to see. "This was my profession cross when I took my final vows," she said. "My people at Laguna made it for me with some very old trade beads."

She stopped. Sister Anne Regina smiled at her and nodded her head.

"In those days we could choose what we wanted for our profession cross," Consolata continued, "but now we can't. We all wear the same thing. I can't wear this anymore, and I want to give it to you."

I was stunned. I could not think what to say. I did not know what to do. I felt the tree, its branches perhaps eighty feet in circumference, soaring above me. I was aware of this, aware of the two sisters watching me. I did not know what to do. Now Sister Anne Regina was nodding and smiling at *me*. So I took the necklace from Consolata. It was a round medallion attached to a strip of soft buckskin. Sky-blue beads covered the medallion, and on top of that, in black beads, were the Greek letters XR. Chi Rho, the first two letters of XRICTOC. Christ. A black arrow curved around the XR and pointed down.

"This means Christ is my protection," Consolata told me. "The arrow. The arrow means protection."

I knew that once Consolata was gone, I would not likely see her again. As I put her profession cross, her gift, around my neck, I felt the tears run down my face. I embraced her and walked back home.

The Last True Apache Chief

Richard knew two San Carlos Apache men very well. One, Clarence Wesley, worked with my husband in the Bureau of Indian Affairs Employment Assistance Office; the other, Britton Goode, regularly dropped into the office over a period of three years and shared Apache beliefs and stories with Richard. The former was sometimes referred to as "the last true Apache chief," and the latter, in my husband's eyes, was "the medicine man."

On December 14, 1972, two years after we came to San Carlos, the reservation marked its 100th anniversary. Richard wondered on that occasion, just how does an Apache "celebrate" 100 years of being a "prisoner of war"? In his mind, all the negative consequences of forcing a people to live in a proscribed area in perpetuity were sufficient to motivate one to bolt from the reservation just as soon as one could; but, his two friends, Clarence and Britton, dearly loved their homeland, and each coped with what they had been given with style, spirit, courage and humor.

In 1971, Richard received a grant from Arizona State University to hold a seminar for the purpose of discussing social and cultural problems on the San Carlos Reservation. Richard used the money to hire two guest speakers. The seminar, which met on four different nights, drew enough people, mostly Apaches, to fill the classroom. They came on three of those nights to hear their own Tony Machukay, who had returned home from Chicago to become the head of the Arizona Commission on Indian Affairs. Tony was a compelling, knowledgeable speaker, but it was something the other guest speaker said that has remained with me to this day. Wayne T. Pratt was

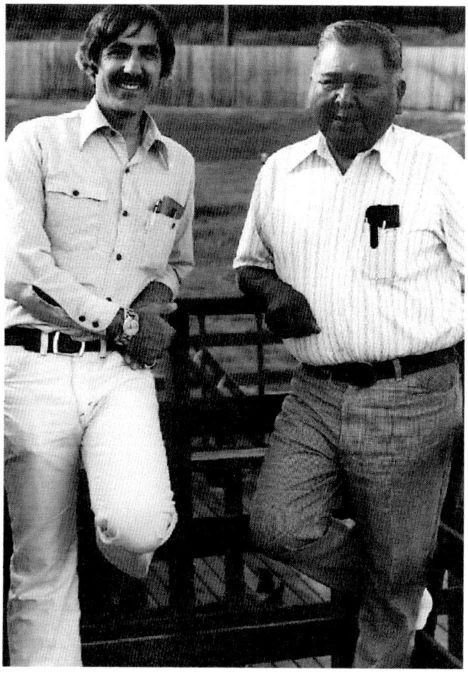

Richard and Clarence Wesley when Mr. Wesley visited us in Denver.

an anthropologist who had retired as assistant chief of the Branch of Education, Bureau of Indian Affairs, U.S. Department of the Interior in Washington, D.C. He finished his presentation with a reference to Clarence Wesley.

"Clarence Wesley was the last true Apache chief," Mr. Pratt said, "because he spoke with authority. He spoke like a chief. And people listened."

Clarence Wesley was born at Calva on the San Carlos Reservation on December 27, 1910. He was born in a wickiup, one of those tents made of animal skins in which Apaches slept when they were nomads. At Phoenix Indian School, he slept in his first bed—and promptly fell out onto the floor, a more comfortable arrangement for him, and one that he kept for months.

He would grow up to be one of the most influential and well-known Native Americans in the United States. Active in tribal politics since 1938, he served as tribal chairman from 1948 to 1954 and again from 1958 to 1962. In 1965 and again in 1966, he served as president of the National Congress of American

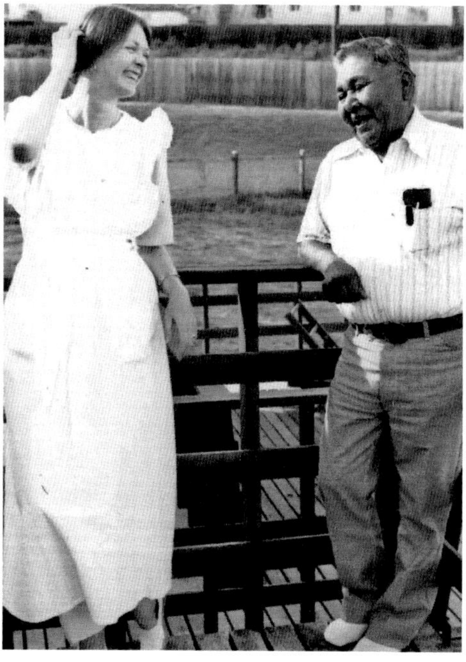

Clarence and I stand on our deck in Denver.

Indians. His executive director during both of his terms was Vine Deloria Jr., Standing Rock Sioux.

Clarence was a cattleman and a working cowboy; he was a singer who conducted Apache religious ceremonials; he was a devout Christian who taught Sunday school at the Lutheran mission. After his retirement, he spent his last years teaching important things to his sixty-four grandchildren. "Apache language, Apache songs, ceremonial dances, Apache medicine, Apache stories and, last but not least," he said, "Apache politics."

Apache politics are fraught with danger.

When we arrived in San Carlos in 1970, Ted Whitebull, the Bureau of Indian Affairs superintendent, told Richard that another person had competed for the job for which Richard had been hired. That person was Clarence Wesley, who was at the time running the BIA Employment Assistance Program for the Hualapai Tribe on the reservation at the far west edge of the Grand Canyon. Richard asked Ted why he had not given the San Carlos job to Clarence, a tribal member who spoke Apache and knew everyone in the community.

"I was embarrassingly ignorant about tribal governance," Richard says, "so Ted explained that Clarence Wesley was a former tribal chairman who had lost that position in an election that had been so contentious and corrupt that the BIA had stepped in and offered him a good federal job at a place far away from San Carlos in the hopes the political climate would cool down."

"Well, Dave," Ted said, "I have spoken to Clarence many times over the last few weeks about the job you have now, and I believe you will hear from him in person very soon."

"And I did," Richard said. "Within the week, Clarence called. I still knew nothing about him. It took many years for me to find out what an important national figure he was in Indian civil rights and education. I did not know he had been president of the National Congress of American Indians, that for twenty years he had been active in tribal government as either chairman or secretary of the San Carlos Tribal Council and that he was frequently asked to testify before Congress on Indian education, self-determination and health and welfare. I did not know any of this when Clarence called me. He was posted four hundred miles from his family and the place he had lived his entire adult life. And now, he said, he was stuck on the Hualapai Reservation. He told me he was living among people he did not understand, had very little work to do and was having a hard time supporting two residences. He had a large family in the Bylas community on the San Carlos Reservation, and it was extremely difficult to make so many trips back home to deal with family emergencies and obligations, as well as the management of his cattle.

"At the end of our conversation, I wanted Clarence to be able to come home. There was a vacant position in our office, and I promised him I would talk to the superintendent about transferring him to San Carlos. I quickly learned how naive I was in making such a promise. When Ted learned what I had said to Clarence, he was clearly agitated. I had not known the last election had been rife with bribery, vandalism and threats of violence. BIA law enforcement personnel were concerned that violence might escalate if the families of the current tribal chairman and Clarence Wesley tried to coexist on 'only' 2,900 square miles of reservation. Ted made his point about how bad relationships were between the two families by telling me of the time he visited the current tribal chairman to gauge how he felt about Clarence's return to San Carlos. In reply to Ted's question, the chairman removed a revolver from a drawer and placed it on top of his desk. There was no more talk about Clarence coming home.

"Now I was really determined to have Clarence on my staff. I proposed to Ted that I visit the chairman and make a case for how valuable Clarence would be to the recruitment and assessment of Apaches who qualified for employment services. I told Ted I would personally monitor Clarence and dissuade him from engaging in tribal politics as long as he worked for the federal government. He would be subject to the provisions of the Hatch Act of 1939, which prohibits federal employees from engaging in partisan politics by bribery, active campaigning for party candidates and misuse of government money and time. Of course, my idea was further proof of my naiveté with respect to both Clarence and tribal politics.

"Ted reluctantly promised to request Clarence's transfer to San Carlos if the chairman agreed with my plan. I was nervous the next day when I met with the chairman and made my case for having Clarence work with me. I held my breath when the chairman opened the middle drawer of his desk. But instead of a gun, he drew out paper and pen. He wrote a note to the superintendent endorsing Clarence's return to San Carlos, 'as long as Mr. Richard David keeps him out of tribal politics.' I recall that I worried from that day forward that I might someday get shot.

"By January of 1971, Clarence was working for the San Carlos Agency. The transition was smooth. With him in the office next door, I could now launch some of the initiatives I had dreamed of before I left Chicago. One thing I wanted to do was to work for and with the tribal government to develop reservation-based programs to help Apaches transition into permanent local employment. I had the promise of the national director of the Employment Assistance Program to provide a limited amount of discretionary funding to test various strategies. With the high incidence of alcoholism on the reservation, I also wanted to encourage the adoption of a joint agreement between tribal, state and federal governments that would address the problem in a unified and systematic manner.

"And finally, my most ambitious goal was to entice commercial enterprises to the reservation. I promoted Joanne Thompson from a secretarial to a technical position, and for two years, Clarence and Joanne carried the load for the Employment Assistance Program while I focused on developing local training and employment, as an alternative to moving Native Americans to major U.S. cities. (I had a vision, even then, of leaving the San Carlos employment program entirely in the hands of Native American professionals.)

"In the meantime, Clarence established a monthly column in the *Arizona Silver Belt* newspaper in Globe, in which he wrote about Apache history and culture but *never* about tribal politics.

"One day, as the election of a new tribal chairman loomed on the horizon, Clarence came into my office and asked if we could talk privately. My friend was distressed that he was unable, as far as he could determine, to be even a spectator in tribal politics. He complained that without the freedom to attend open tribal government meetings, he would be the least informed member of the tribe. I had anticipated this problem and had reread the Hatch Act to be certain of my position. I told Clarence that if he took official annual leave he would be free to attend open tribal council meetings. 'The chairman won't like seeing you there,' I told him, 'but as long as you are not campaigning for yourself or another candidate, or otherwise disrupting proceedings, you are entitled to be there. If I have a leave slip with your signature when you attend council meetings, there should be no problem.'

"Clarence began attending tribal council meetings, including special sessions. A short time later, I was approached outside the Peridot Trading Post by an Apache man who I did not know well. 'Aren't you Mr. Wesley's boss?' he asked. He told me I should not allow Clarence to attend council meetings because he was not an elected councilman. When I defended Clarence's right to be there the man said, 'I believe we will have to assassinate Mr. Wesley.'

"A woman who I think was the man's mother was sitting in a nearby car listening to this conversation. She stuck her head out the car window and yelled, 'You talk just like Mr. Wesley. I guess we will have to assassinate you, too.'

"No one witnessed this incident, and I returned to my office to report it. Clarence and the superintendent were out, so I walked over to the police department to talk to Federal Special Agent Youngdeer. I described the confrontation and asked what precautions I should take. 'Make a formal statement in my presence, immediately,' he said. 'You will sign it and then you and I will find Mr. Wesley and warn him. And finally, I would advise you to arm yourself until the election is over.'

"I told Agent Youngdeer I did not own a firearm and that the few times in high school when I tried target shooting I never hit anything. Would a hunting knife suffice? He laughed and said, 'Ask Jim Foxx [a BIA social worker] if you can borrow one of his revolvers.'

"I stopped by Jim's house that evening, told him about the events of the day and that Youngdeer had advised me to carry a weapon. Jim loaned me his nickel-plated Colt 38 Special with the ivory grip. He also gave me an old tobacco pouch containing ten cartridges. He recommended that I go out to the abandoned stone quarry and do a little target practice. I never did. For six months, I carried the pistol in my briefcase. I placed it on top of papers so that it would be displayed when I put the open case on a low table next to my desk. I stored the cartridges on the top shelf of the hall closet at home.

"Clarence, being the old hand he was, dismissed the threat as 'just San Carlos politics.' After the election, he and I would laugh at the thought of me throwing an unloaded Colt 38—with an ivory grip—at an assailant.

"Before we departed San Carlos in 1975, Clarence slaughtered one of his steers for the farewell barbecue that would be held down by the San Carlos River bed. Clarence visited us twice in Colorado, and we corresponded until the end of his life. His letters reveal how many times he tried to persuade the Bureau of Indian Affairs area office to bring me back to San Carlos. I am incredibly proud to have been called a good friend and brother by the last true Apache chief."

The Medicine Man

Christmas Day 1972 was the first time Richard and I had been invited into the home of an Apache. We were in Britton Goode's sixty-foot double-wide mobile home—across the street and down a way from our house—celebrating the fact that Britton's son, Eldad, was back in Globe High School after having been suspended because he refused to cut off his long hair. At the time of the celebration, I knew only that Britton was a former medicine man, a traditional healer, who, at the urging of his wife, Marie, and the evangelical missionaries at the independent church to which she belonged, had given up his Apache ways to become a Christian. Furthermore, because Britton was one of the few Apaches literate and fluent in both Apache and English, he had been a major participant in the translation of the New Testament into the Apache language. At the time, I had no way of knowing that Britton was the son of a famous scout and medicine man who had tracked Geronimo for General George Crook or that Britton himself was well known in some academic circles. (In 2001, Richard would find a paper published in the *American Ethnologist* by David Samuels, an anthropology professor at the University of Massachusetts–Amherst, which was prefaced by the following words: "In this article, I concentrate on the place names compiled by Britton Goode [1911–1981], a Western Apache linguist and historian.")

Earlier that year when Britton had appeared at the Bureau of Indian Affairs agency, Richard assumed he was there to see Clarence Wesley, and he was surprised when Britton walked into his own office and said, "Mr. David, what do you know about us Apaches?"

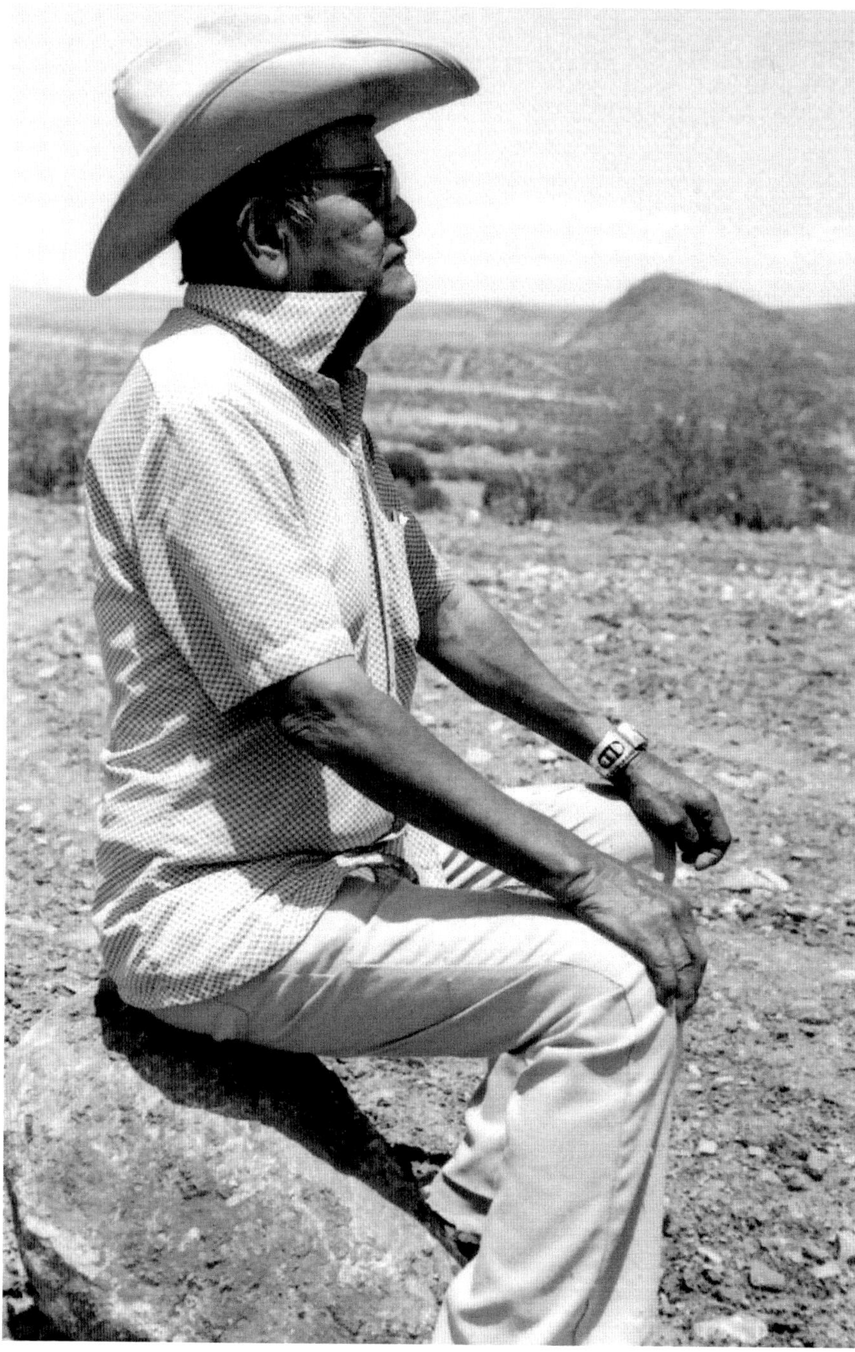

Britton Goode at Dripping Springs.

Having read Dee Brown's recently published *Bury My Heart at Wounded Knee*, a book sympathetic to the Apaches and complimentary of their tactics in waging guerrilla warfare against the United States Cavalry, Richard told Britton that he believed the Apaches' struggle against oppression was completely justified, and though outnumbered in battles, they had been formidable combatants.

Britton thought for a moment and then said, "Would you like to know more about us?"

"Yes, I would," Richard said. "Of course I would. May I take notes?"

"OK," Britton said. "That way I can check to see that you got it right."

For the next three years, Britton would stop by Richard's office every month or so to instruct him in the ways of the Apaches. And true to his word, Britton did look at Richard's notes to make certain he "got it right."

BRITTON'S LIFE

"I am the son of an old Apache scout, Robert Go'd. He trailed the Chiricahua Apache, Geronimo, under General Crook. He and my beloved mother, Emma, raised seven of us in a wickiup with no electric light, no tableware and no spring bed. We slept on a straw mattress on the ground. There was nothing to enjoy like we have today. We wore one set of clothes until they were worn out, and our toes stuck out of our shoes. Mother would do laundry at the river edge, and she used a flat rock for a washboard. We would get little to eat, but we were happy that our old father drew a government pension of thirty-five dollars a month. No complaints.

"I did all I could to learn the white man's language and ways, but my old folks always rejected my proposals. One time I wanted to go to Albuquerque Indian School, but my folks said 'Why should you go to such a place? Many things happen.' Next, I wanted to go to Phoenix Indian School. I prepared and packed my things and went to where the Model T would take off for Phoenix. They called the names of the pupils going but my name did not get called. Now, I have only poor grammar and vocabulary."*

The next time Britton came to Richard's office, Richard asked him how Apaches described the seasons of the year.

*. Britton Goode, "Precious Memory of the Goodes," handwritten, unpublished notes.

"OK," Britton said. "Spring is everything waking up, and autumn is everything ripening. Summer is the hot season, and winter is the cool season."

"Ah, come on, Britton!" Richard said. "That's it?"

"That is *sure* it," Britton replied and laughed. But he then spent the next hour working out how to describe the twelve months from an Apache perspective. He would think about each month, say something in Apache and then translate the Apache into English. These are Britton's words:

January, Time of the white spot on the high mountain
February, Time of owl-hooting heard in the daytime
March, Time of cleaning trees
April, Time of beginning new leaves
May, Time of big leaves
June, Time of blossoms on trees
July, Time of food spoiling
August, Time to eat plants
September, Time when corn is fully ripened
October, Time of people moving closer together
November, Time of melting snow for water
December, Time of cold wind around campfire.

"Did the people who came to this continent bring this calendar of twelve months with them?" Britton asked. Richard nodded.

"I guess that's what the problem is!" Britton quipped.

From then on, Britton brought Richard's "lesson" in the form of handwritten notes. He would have Richard make a photocopy of the notes so he could "study for the test."

Britton told Richard that other Indian tribes were afraid of the "war-making" Apaches. "One time," he said, "my late wife, Marie, and I made a trip to Hopi land to see our missionary friends, Fred Johnson and his wife. They gave us good hospitality and they took us around the mesas, and we came to a place where three old Hopi men were taking a sun bath against a wall. Fred began talking to the old men in their own language, and every time he finished a statement they would say *ha'oh*, which means *isn't that so?* in Hopi, and *yes* in Apache. At one point they all had a big laugh. Later, I asked what that big laugh was about.

"I introduced you as Apaches," Fred said, "and one of the old men said to keep you away because they were afraid of Apaches. He said that many years ago, the Apaches missed the Hopis on their mesa because the Hopis' atomic bomb kept them away!"

(The Hopis were making a joke of what may have been a very real fear. The name *Apache* is probably a corruption by the Spanish colonialists of *'a pacŭ*, the Zuni word for enemy.)*

One day in July 1974, Britton came to Richard's office and asked him if he would like to take a ride. "Where are we going?" Richard asked. "To Dripping Springs," Britton told him. So off they went, Britton and Richard, into the desert without water or food. Richard drove. Sixty miles of surfaced highway and ten miles of dirt road later, they walked into the Dripping Springs Wash. Richard had his new Pentax camera and a telephoto lens. He hoped to take a picture of the actual Dripping Springs, which, according to the fourth creation story, had impregnated the only woman, the only human, left on earth after the big flood.

The spring to which Britton led Richard was in a small cave about five feet deep and four or five feet high. Although no water dripped, the floor of the cave was wet with fresh water from the spring below. Richard did not photograph the spring; it was a religious site, he explained later, and he did not want to defile it. Britton walked away and sat down on a small boulder. He sat very still and stared off into the desert. Richard wondered if he was praying. Quietly, he took Britton's picture, and then, he told me, he reeled off the remaining thirty-five frames with shots of the desert and surrounding mountains. The picture of Britton is the only image that came out of that roll of film. The other thirty-five images were overexposed.

Britton wrote Richard many times after we left San Carlos. In 1980, we received a Christmas card on the front of which Britton had written, "Job 29: 2–3." The quotation from the King James Bible reads: "Oh that I were as in months past, as in the days when God preserved me; When his candle shined upon my head, and when by his light I walked through darkness."

In January 1981, Britton wrote to say he had cancer of the jaw: "Rich, don't let that worry you," he assured him. "Happiness does not always stay with man, or for ever."

In February, Britton wrote to say he was back in Phoenix Indian Hospital and to urge Richard to write up the lessons he had once given him. "I know you will do better on history because you can read my broken English and understand my writing." Britton wanted his "epic" to be published.

---

*. Karl Jacoby, *Shadows at Dawn: A Borderlands Massacre and the Violence of History* (New York: Penguin Press, 2008), 285.

In June, we heard from Britton for the last time. He was back in San Carlos, after having undergone surgery. "I promised to visit you in June but I am afraid I will not until later." He sends us "God's protection" and signs off "Goodbye *Yaalan*." He died in December.

"Now that I have repeated some of the stories Britton Goode told me," Richard says, "I wish he were still alive so I could ask him one last question: 'Well, old friend, did I get it right?'"

Britton's Epic: Apache Pride*

The United States government spared us a place to live, where we are now, which was a part of the happy land where our ancestors roamed. All ancient Apache trails are lonesome trails. Apaches would travel north, south, east and west and sing love songs so the distances would never be too far for them.

The original name of the San Carlos Apaches is *substantial food grinder*. Before foreigners were known, the Southern Apache headquartered at Old San Carlos, a place called *bare ground extending toward the water or river*. The Apache people used to live in riches. They had plenty of ancient foods such as seeds, nuts, green plants and mescal. They could eat almost anything, but being a superstitious people, they did not eat snakes, lizards, frogs, owls or anything from the hawk kingdom. We traveled great distances and lived in many places: red tulip pond and valley, blue pond valley, mescal mountain, rough timber mountain, clay pool, big cottonwood spring, antelope garden, high water river, red streaked river and rugged canyon.

There is a year-round bird that has a big nest. This little bird, the Verdin, is about the size of a bat. It is well known to all Apaches. The doorway of its nest, especially in winter, is so small that it almost closes when the small little bird enters at night. All sorts of feathers are caught on the sides of the opening. The Apaches gather these feathers and put them under the head

---

*. Britton Goode, "Britton's Epic, Apache Pride," compiled from photocopies of notes shown to Richard David by Britton Goode between 1972 and 1975.

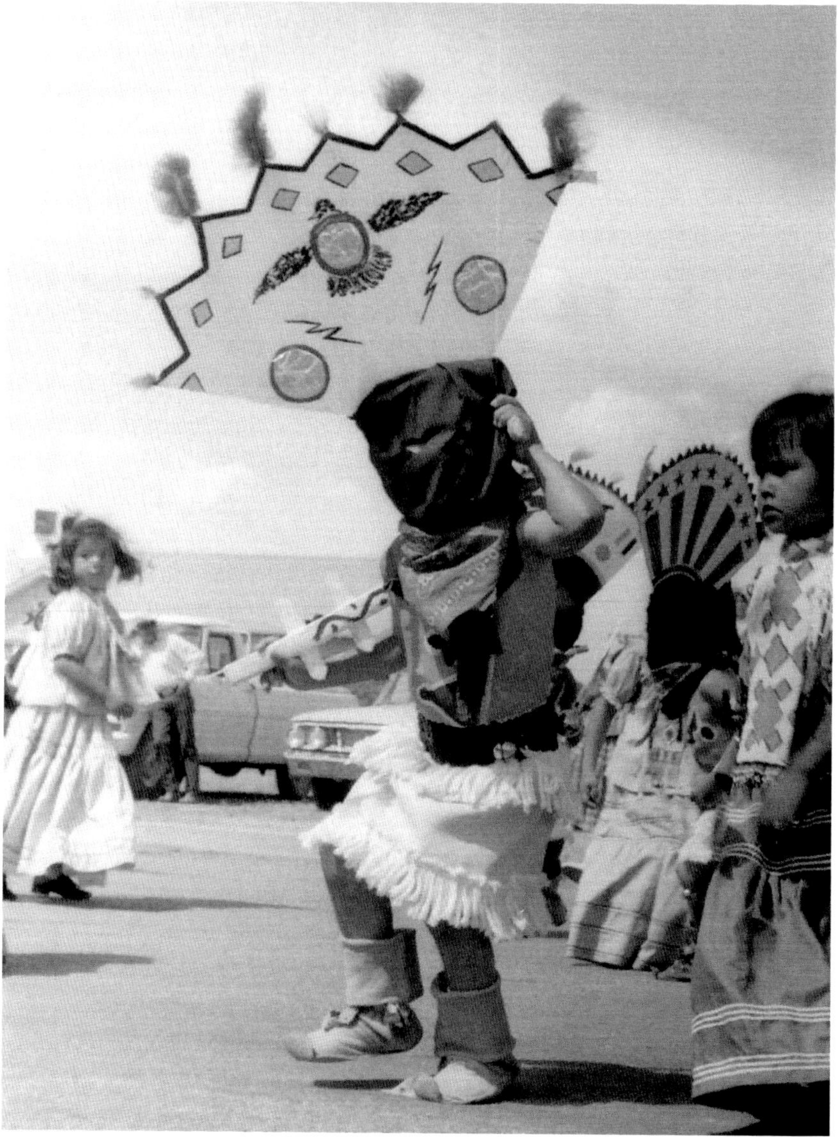

Little Gáán dancers and little girls in camp dresses perform in a parade in San Carlos.

of the baby in the cradleboard so the baby can go fast to sleep and make no noise that our enemy can hear.

Gambel's quail run fast, and they are frisky. If an Apache kills a quail, the feet are cut off and used to tickle the feet of a newborn baby so it will walk before its time.

MR. COYOTE

Coyote and his cousin, Grey Fox, came long ago to the present site of San Carlos. It was then a place where white people lived. When they arrived at this place they saw an image, like a scarecrow, that seemed to be made of tar or something of a sticky substance. The old coyote was a little afraid of the image, so he decided to hit it. When he swung at the image with his front paw, it stuck fast. That made him mad, so he swung with the other front paw, and the same thing happened. Finally, all of his legs were stuck and he could not get away. Grey Fox just went away and left his cousin. The next day white men found Mr. Coyote and they pulled him down. He was so sticky that they boiled water and dropped him in it. The hot water not only took off his sticky substance, but it also took off all of his hair and turned his skin red. Old Mr. Coyote started his journey home when the white men released him. On his way up the mountain he came across his cousin. Grey Fox called out "Hey, Cousin! Where did you get those beautiful red clothes?"

THE CREATION STORIES

The First Story

The Apaches believe that in the beginning the earth was like a balloon floating all around. It was not steady. There were four different colored airs, or winds, which were used to make braces for the earth. The black wind did not work too well, but the green one almost made the earth settle down. The yellow wind nearly did the job, but the white wind held the earth very well. Later, the stars were made. Mr. Coyote said he wanted to make some stars for himself, because he thought they were so pretty.

"I like that dipper," he said, "so I will make one with stars." And that is why our people call those stars the Coyote Dipper.

Apaches say the blue color of the sky is God, so he is everywhere at the same time. Like the Christians, who talk about God being "up there," the Apaches talk about the "one who sits beyond." Apaches believe there is a god and that there are intercessors. The most important intercessor is the sun. That is why Apaches pray toward the east in the morning and turn toward the sun as it moves from east to west. The sun is not God, but it can help answer prayers. God does not send his word directly, but he sends it through the sun.

The Second Story

This is a story told by Apaches of old. Many years ago there were Mountain Spirits, called Gáán in Apache, who lived inside the earth. After a while they began to die, and this went on unceasingly until finally they decided to move to the top of the earth and live like human beings. For many years the Gáán lived like the rest of us. They built houses and cities, the ruins of which you can see today on the tops of mountains and hills. One funny thing is that the anthropologists dig up skeletons that they think are old human beings, and they do not know that they have really found the remains of the Gáán. That is pretty funny.

The Gáán lived on earth for a very long time. They did dances that brought blessings and healing to the people. Eventually, the Gáán desired and sought a better world. One day the rainbow came down and formed a staircase that the Mountain Spirits used to ascend to a higher world. They paused to remind the people they were leaving something behind. "What we have been able to do," they said, "you also can do." The people then began the dances of the Gáán so that they could bring the blessings upon themselves. As far as we know, the Gáán, the Mountain Spirits, now live in a better world, and the dances that Apache people perform are the ones we have learned from the Mountain Spirits.

The Third Story

One day a big flood came, like the one in the Bible, and three women prepared a hollow log with provisions and a metate to grind the corn. They got into the log and sealed it up. They floated for many years. They would pound on the side of the log to determine if the water had receded. When the water receded, the women unsealed the log, and when they got out, they saw tracks in the mud. They followed the tracks and found the animal that had made the tracks. They asked the creature, "Are you a human being?" But the creature did not answer. No men survived the flood.

The Fourth Story, a Variation

Apache people tell this story about how they came to be. After the big flood there was only one human left, and it was a woman. Her Apache name meant "never die in old age." She was like any person, except that when she got old and near the age of death, she would become young again. We don't know how she did this.

The woman was able to have a baby without a husband. First, she exposed herself to the first rays of the sun and then to the wind and, finally, to dripping water. When her female offspring was born, the woman believed that the dripping water had produced the infant. When the girl came of age, her mother told her to practice all of the same things she herself had done to conceive.

For discipline, the daughter was instructed to tend the garden. The girl, while working in the garden, saw a racer snake, and she asked it, "Are you a man?" This happened three times. On the fourth sighting of the snake, a man appeared in the garden, and he had intercourse with the girl. When the girl returned to her mother she told of seeing the snake four times, but she did not mention the man. Nevertheless, her mother knew what had happened. The daughter had a male child. At the beginning he had an Apache name that meant "having arrived in a flash." When he became a man he had another name.

YAALAN

We now see our children using a foreigner's language rather than their native tongue. We have entered a fast changing world. It seems that some of our people have entered the white man's educational warfare. I wonder how it will be in the next hundred years? Where is the end destination? Will there be no more Apaches?

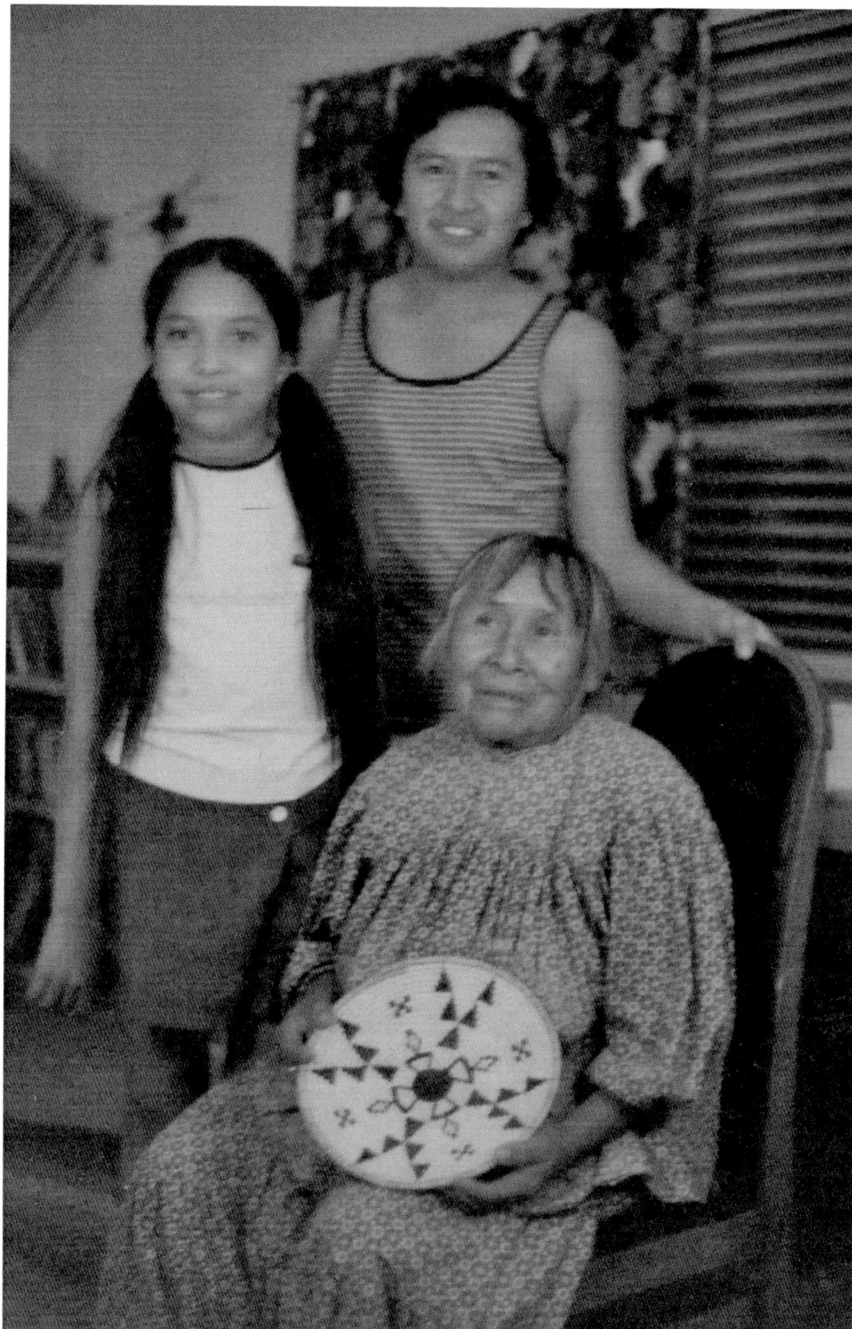

Gusta Thompson, one of the greatest of the Apache basket weavers, holds the first basket she made for us. She is shown in our house with her grandchildren, Bernadette and Herbert Stevens.

Journal Notes 1973–75

The Artist

Herbert Stevens, the Apache artist, looks splendid, as always. He wears knee-high buckskin boots (his own creation) and a fringed and beaded buckskin shirt. Herbert and my cousin Louie (also an artist), who is visiting from Los Angeles for Easter, are helping me make the chasuble Father Bart will wear at the Easter vigil. We have cut from cloth a saguaro cactus to sew on the front of the chasuble and, for the back, a yellow and orange rising sun with the words "The Dawn of Joy." We laugh about how we are going to make Father Bart look like a hippie priest. Father Bart is a very traditional priest—no early evening vigil for him. Near midnight, Herbert, Louie and I stand with the rest of the congregation outside the front door of the church and watch as Father Bart kindles the Easter fire from a large brazier. From his candle we light our own candles and follow him into the church.

Herbert's grandmother, Gusta Thompson, is one of the last great Apache weavers. She does not make burden baskets but, rather, tightly woven food baskets and, occasionally, a rare, tall olla. We are lucky to have one of her food baskets. Herbert brought Gusta to our house when the basket was finished so we could take a picture of her holding it. One day I ask Herbert to take me to his grandmother's house where she is weaving another basket for us. This basket will be tall and have figures of horses, people and saguaro cacti. But when we arrive, Gusta will not talk to me. She is angry; she will not look at me. She does not like that I am at her house, that her grandson has brought me there. I am embarrassed because not only have I gone to an Apache home without being invited, I have persuaded my friend to take me there. Gusta and Herbert speak in Apache, and we leave. Richard and I buy the beautiful basket from Herbert when it is finished, and we enter it in the Arizona State Fair. Of course it wins a blue ribbon. Everything Gusta weaves wins a blue ribbon.

One day, Herbert brings me a small eagle plume. The plume is white and very, very soft. Herbert tells me that the next time I have a baby it would be a good thing for me to put that plume on the top of my baby's Apache cradleboard. That eagle plume will bring blessings to the baby. I thank him with all my heart and promise him I will do exactly that.

Burden Basket

Roe stands on the front porch and shows me a miniature burden basket, no more than three inches high. The basket is finely woven from tiny lengths of brown, tan and dark red cotton willow. Sixteen tin cones made from Crisco cans dangle from strips of soft buckskin.

"Five dollars for you," he says.

"That's not much." I'm skeptical.

"You're a friend," he insists, his perpetual grin, wide-open eyes, encouraging me. His remarkably smooth skin contrasts oddly with his gray hair, half hidden beneath a battered felt hat. In his dirty Levi's and torn leather shoes, he walks every day with his wife, who wears a long, red camp dress, between our house and the church. Whenever I see him, we stop to talk and he tells me about his experiences in France in World War II. He has the ever-ready cheerfulness of a professional con man. But I like Roe, and I ignore my intuition and give him five dollars. I jiggle the tiny object (the tin cones ring like little bells), and I think how sweet it will look hanging with Celena Perry's full-sized burden basket on the wall next to the bookshelf.

A month later, a tribal policeman comes to my door, asks me if I have purchased a miniature basket from Roe and shows me a subpoena to appear in tribal court.

On the appointed morning, I put the basket in a paper sack and walk over to the little courtroom behind the police station, where I am told to sit on the front bench. I am the only white person in the room. Next to me sits the

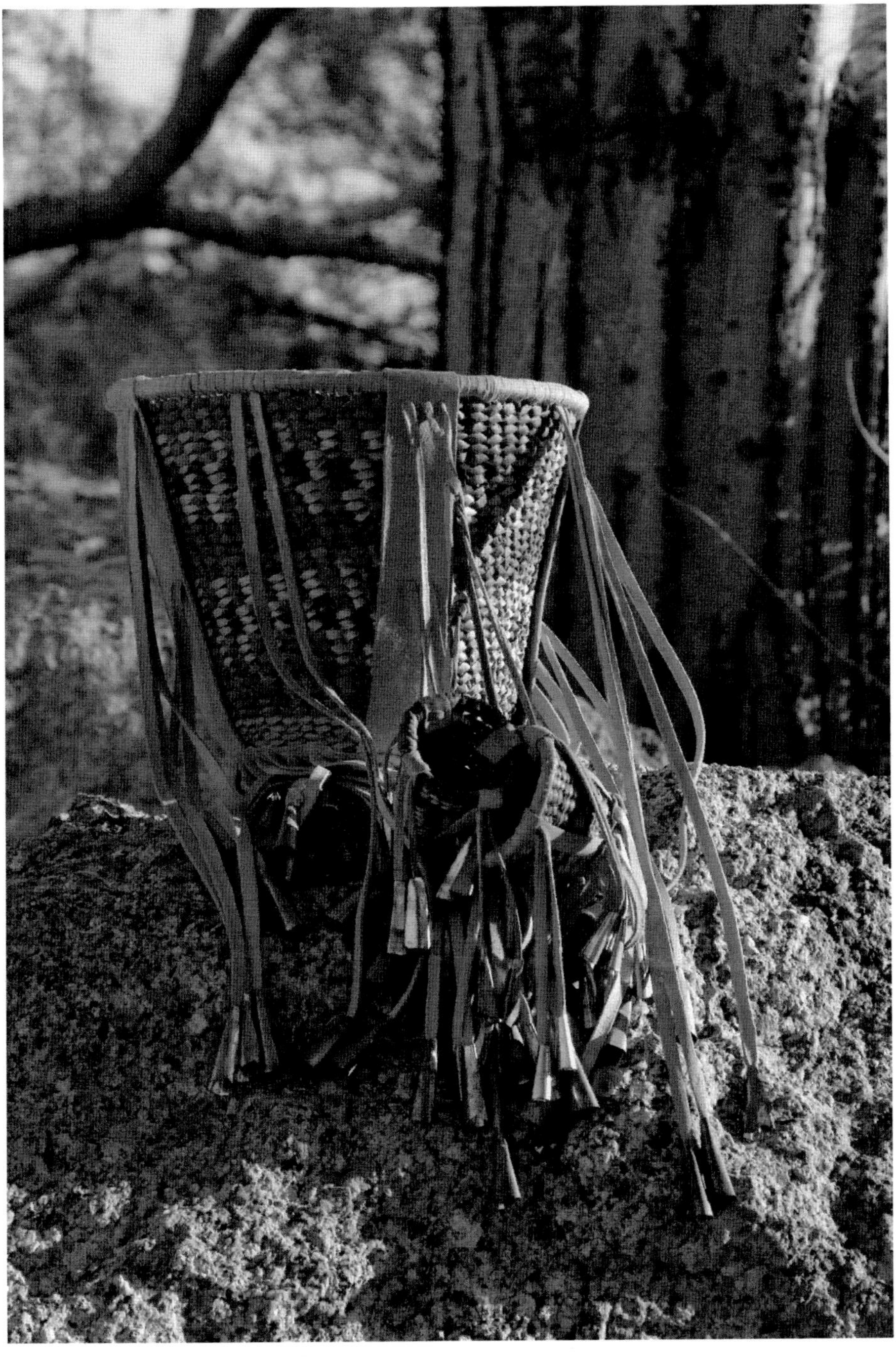

The large Apache burden basket and the tiny ones attached to it were made by Celena Perry.

tribal secretary; it is her daughter's basket, given to her by her godmother at her Sunrise Ceremony, that I have purchased.

"I think we are ready to begin," says the judge. A policeman opens a door at the front of the room, and out steps Roe. He waves to me and smiles. The judge lectures Roe on stealing. The judge also lectures me on buying stolen property, thereby contributing to the habit of an alcoholic. Is Roe an alcoholic? I never thought so, but the judge seems to enjoy his role of ethical teacher (preacher?), and he goes on and on. Finally, he finishes his exhortation and I return the basket and Roe returns my five dollars. He winks as he places the bill in my hand. I laugh. I can't help it. The judge looks at me sternly.

Dream

She said she killed her husband in self-defense, and the jury agreed. But when she has a dream in which "the old ones" of the Apache people visit her, she knows she has received an important message. In her dream she is out on the desert near San Carlos, and it looks as it always does except for one thing: it is both day and night at the same time. "Light and dark mixed together," she says. Many people are there, walking around, and she knows they are dead. All of them carry watering cans, and they very carefully water each little cactus, each little plant.

"They must do this forever," she tells Richard. "They must do this to make up for all the bad things they did while they were alive."

Marie

"I don't know her name," my Navajo friend Marie Duncan tells me in her quick, nearly breathless English, each syllable clipped off at the end more abruptly than in the softer, less accented speech of her Apache husband and son. "Everyone just calls her the Old Woman Across the River. She cured me of my headaches."

I have never seen the Old Woman Across the River, but I have heard stories of her healing powers. The fundamentalist Christian missionaries call her a witch. Nevertheless, people who have tried everyone else without success (the medicine man, the Indian Health doctors) make their way to her little house across the San Carlos River and sit on the ground in front of that house while she determines the source of their illnesses. The Old Woman, as with most practitioners of the healing arts, accepts payment for her services, but, judging from what I have heard of her lifestyle, her fees can't be very high.

"Tell me about her," I ask Marie. "How old is she? And how did she cure you?"

"No one knows her age," Marie says. "My headaches got so bad that my husband took me over to her house and told me not to talk but to listen to whatever she said. So she looked at me for a long time, and after a while she spoke. She said that once when I was playing basketball in high school the ball smashed into my glasses. They broke and a piece of glass went into my eye. And that was why I had headaches."

"Did that happen to you in high school?"

"I got hit in the face with a basketball once, and my glasses broke, but I never thought about getting glass in my eye."

"Did you go to the hospital, after the Old Woman told you that, to see if there really was a piece of glass in your eye?"

"No, I didn't, because I haven't had any headaches after I saw the Old Woman. So, I think she just healed me."

One day, Marie arrives at my house and hands me a pair of silver and turquoise earrings. They look like chandeliers; in each earring, seven small oval pieces of turquoise set in silver dangle from a single turquoise at the top. I am surprised, delighted, by Marie's unexpected gift. She tells me her great-aunt gave her these earrings for her college graduation. How can she bear to part with them?

Two years later, Marie's husband, Eugene, gives me a farewell gift he made for me in the silversmith class of our community college extension program: a silver necklace, a choker, set with five beautifully matched turquoise oval stones, each one over half an inch long. I know the blue stone is a blessing stone for the Navajos, the "Walk in Beauty" stone, as I think of it. I will be blessed by these gifts from Marie and Eugene for the rest of my life.

JOHANNA

Johanna gives Richard a necklace made of polished green peridot stones at the end of which hangs a large peridot pendant encased in silver. The stones were found in the ground near the Peridot Trading Post. Johanna thanks Richard for helping her son go to junior college when he was ill. She thanks us for attending his funeral. "I wish, with these Peridot stones," she writes, "you find all happy days ahead."

The peridot is the birthstone of August, my birthstone, and because Richard wears only a small silver medal of St. Francis of Assisi, I become the recipient of that beautiful necklace. I wear it until it falls apart.

Joanne

Joanne Thompson, Richard's assistant, who is a member of the Pima Tribe from the Gila River Indian Community, gives Richard a large flat basket woven by an artist from her tribe. The basket portrays the man in the maze

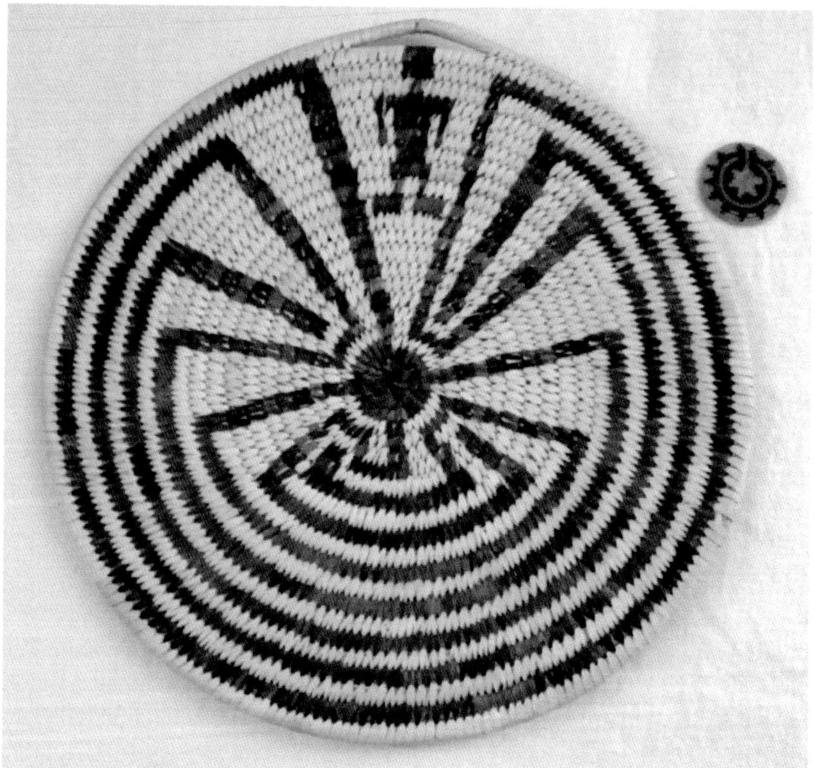

The Pima man in the maze basket and the miniature horsehair basket were gifts to Richard from Joanne Thompson.

or, as it is also called, the maze of life pattern. Later she gives him a miniature of that basket, but this tiny basket, woven of horsehair, is no more than an inch and a quarter in diameter. I feel overwhelmed by the generosity of Native Americans.

GOOD WORKS

Joan and Arnold Gass, with their children, J.J. and Corey, have left the reservation for San Diego. Dr. Gass has been with the Indian Health Service for three years, and he wants to finish a residency in internal medicine. Later he will become associate chief of staff at the VA Hospital and, after that, teach at the University of California medical school. Joan will start an exchange program between schoolchildren from San Diego and the San Carlos Reservation. After a lot of preparation on both sides, about fifty sixth graders from San Diego will live in Apache homes for a week and the same number of children from San Carlos will live with families in San Diego. The exchange program will run for fifteen years, and it will win a national Freedom Foundation Award.

Ellen Kryc, Dr. Joe's wife, is on a mission: she is determined to build up the very small public library that was established a couple of years ago in a small, vacant, tufa stone building on the main street. Working with the tribal council and the BIA, she has procured funding for a librarian. She's brought library science students from the University of Arizona to train the Apache librarian and her assistants in the Dewey Decimal System. She's obtained books through donations from the Gila County Library, persuaded the bookmobile to visit outlying areas of the reservation and, perhaps best of all, has begun a children's reading room. Is there anything Ellen hasn't thought of?

GODCHILD

We have a new godson, Richard and I, a newborn Apache baby who is the son of Dorothy Yellow Eyes and the grandchild of Martha Machukay. I hold George at his baptism at the Catholic mission. A few years after we leave San Carlos, Father Bart will write to tell us that George possesses something wonderful: a kind and good character.

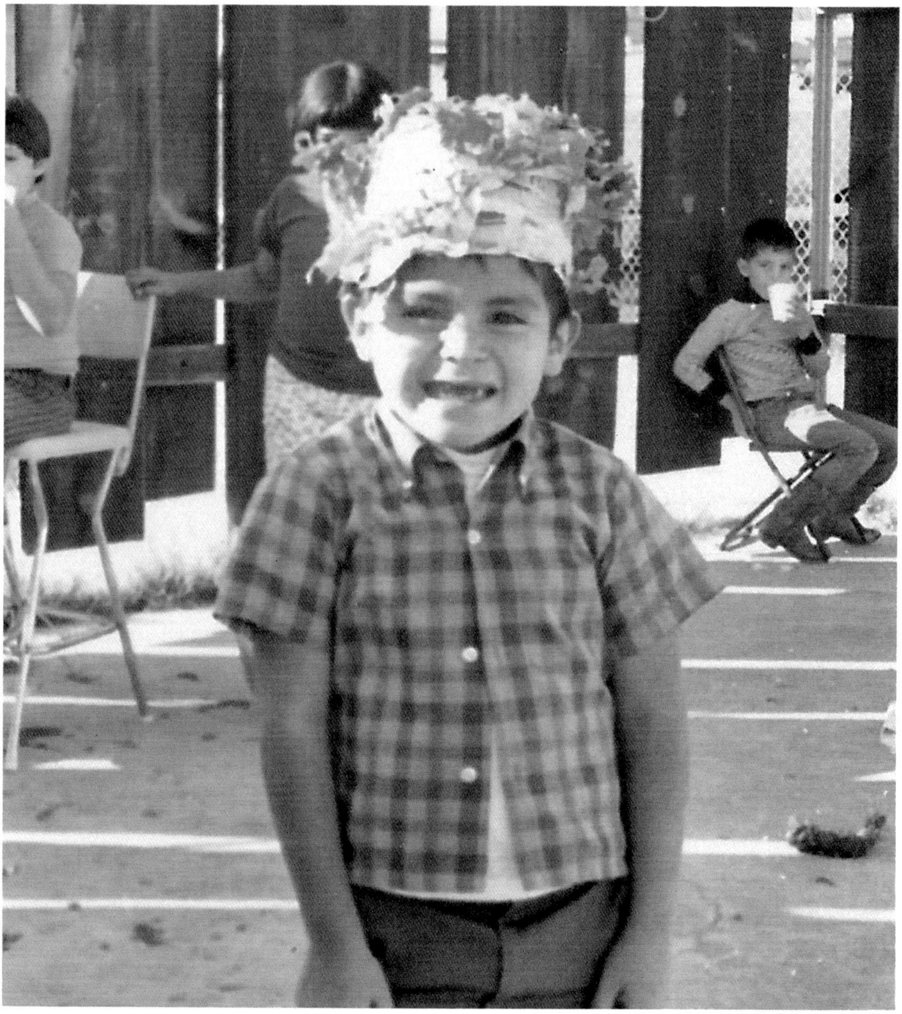

One of the guests at Patrick's birthday party wears part of the broken piñata for a hat.

BRIAN

Patrick and Chris are in their bedroom playing pool with their friend Brian Patten. I am back there trying to dust the furniture. Brian is a skinny little boy with a crew cut. Suddenly, he puts down the pool cue and runs to the window. "Look!" he says, jumping up and down and grinning at us over his shoulder. "Look!" He points to a bird in the tree. "A Baltimore oriole!"

RESCUE

I look out the front door, and I'm startled to see Noelle leading Brother José up our sidewalk. He's bent over, and he walks slowly. Together, Noelle and I help him up the three steps to the veranda and into the house where he sits down in the rocking chair. I bring him a glass of water and ask him if he's all right, but he doesn't answer. I call Father Bart, who sounds very relieved. "I didn't know where Brother José had gone," he tells me. "I've been looking for him all over the place. I'm afraid I will have to take him to Santa Barbara," he says, meaning the Franciscan retirement home. "I'm so happy Noelle found him."

BEAR CUBS

Christopher's third-grade class has gone to Tucson to the Arizona-Sonora Desert Museum on a field trip, but Christopher is not with them. His teacher told him he has lost that privilege because of "talking and disrupting" the class. But Chris will see something better than desert tortoises. When Richard comes home for lunch he says there are twin bear cubs at the tribal police station. Their mother was shot by some firefighters at the garbage dump up at Point of Pines on the northern part of the reservation. Later, the ranger found the cubs and brought them to San Carlos. Richard, Chris, Noclle and I walk to the station to see them.

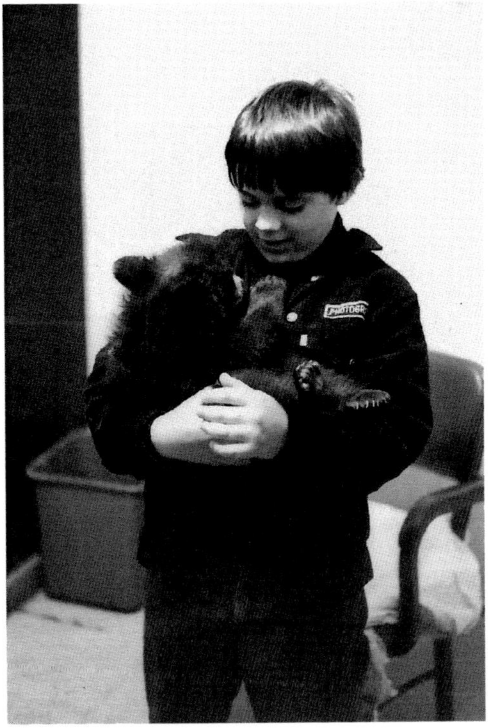

Christopher holds the orphaned baby black bear.

"Poor, poor babies," cries Noelle.

The policeman tells us that someone from the Phoenix Zoo

will be here tomorrow to pick up the cubs. Noelle wants to know if the bears will live at the zoo forever.

One of the jail cells has been converted to a nursery. On the floor, the two black bears, the size of half-grown German Shepherds, tumble around, nibble at legs and ears, slap each other with clumsy paws. The dispatcher bends down, picks up one of the cubs and places it in Noelle's arms. For a second the bear is quiet and Noelle stares at him. Then he begins to wriggle.

"Here, Mommy," says Noelle. I take the cub from her, cuddle my face against his soft, bristly fur, much the way Noelle does with her teddy bear at home. There is a difference: five claws, already thick, alarmingly sharp, scrape across my arm.

Christopher takes up the other twin and cradles him, belly-up, like a human baby. They gaze at each other, and I am struck by how much they look alike: glossy dark hair tumbles over big dark eyes. The cub's paw fits perfectly into Christopher's hand. Chris smiles, and the baby lifts his mouth and latches onto Christopher's chin and sucks.

"Hey, Dad, it tickles," Chris says. He wiggles his head, but the bear hangs on.

"He thinks you're his mama, Christopher," Noelle says.

Words

brother, my **shik'isn**
(man to man);
shilah *(woman to man);*
my older brother **shidee,**
shidee ishkiin, shinágé;
my younger brother **shidizhé**

brother-in-law, my **shiyį́***

The short gray-haired man walking briskly up to my house must be David Seegmiller from Eastern Arizona College in Thatcher, I thought as I opened the door.

"Sonja David?" He smiled. "I'm so glad you've decided to do this. I'm afraid we can't pay very well…" He stopped suddenly and looked up at the iron chandeliers. "My goodness! Your house! It's wonderful! It's like something right out of the *High Chaparral* TV series."

I liked him already. He wanted to know how long we'd lived in the old house, and I told him we had moved in a few months earlier. I asked him to sit down and offered him iced tea or coffee.

"I'd love a plain old glass of water," he said.

"What do I have to do?" I asked, after I'd brought him his water and refilled my own coffee mug.

---

*. White Mountain Apache Cultural Center, *Western Apache Dictionary*, 1972.

"Set up classes, get teachers, register students. I believe there's a lot more interest here than people think. We really want to make this extension program on the reservation a lot bigger."

"What classes did you offer last year?"

"English, math, typing. Basic stuff. Getting folks through the GED. But you can add other things. Whatever you want. We can use the public school. The art teacher would like to teach a class in ceramics."

"What about native crafts?" I asked. "There's a wonderful Apache basket weaver, a Navajo rug weaver, even a silversmith. And, hey! There's a famous mechanic married to one of the Indian Health nurses! He worked on cars at the Indianapolis 500. Maybe we could get him to teach auto mechanics."

"Terrific! Whatever folks want. Just as long as you sign up at least seven students for each class—and, of course, get temporary state certification for the teachers. Not hard to do. I'll show you how to go about it."

"Apache language?" I asked.

"Oh, yes, by all means. If you can find someone to do it."

"Perhaps Reverend Bunney would be willing," I said. "I've heard he not only speaks Apache but that he reads and writes it as well. I do know that he and several Apaches translated the New Testament."

"Perfect!" he said. "And then you, yourself, might like to teach written communication."

"I might."

"It's called a possessive pronoun," I told the adults seated before me. They looked respectful but puzzled. They were bilingual, having learned English as schoolchildren, but they had signed up for my class, I discovered, because they wanted to improve their written skills. Putting words on paper, some of them told me, made them nervous.

"I'm sorry, Sonja, I just can't do it when I have to write it out."

"Don't say you're sorry," I would plead, shamed by their embarrassment. "If I could speak Apache as well as you speak English…"

I had never taught such eager students: Vernon, a rising young tribal employee; Riley, grave and courteous; his wife, Leah; Leah's sister, Agnes (the mother of the pallbearer, David, who was related to Geronimo); bright, good-natured Percy (the youngest member of the class); the Navajo, Dennis; my good friend Ambrose; and finally, Raleigh, who fixed broken stoves and made me laugh.

"Look," I tried again. "Possessive pronouns. In your language they're not separated from the noun. It's all one word. For example, in Apache, my brother is all one word. *Shilaa.* Which, of course, is the way you say it if you're a woman. I realize there's a different way to say it if you're a man, but I haven't learned it yet. How would a man say it?"

No one answered, which was unusual.

"OK," I went on. "*Shilaa.* My brother. The *shi* is the same as *my* in English. We call the *shi*—or *my*—a possessive pronoun because it shows who possesses the brother. The *laa* would be the noun. *Shilaa, shilaa,*" I rattled on, feeling extraordinarily pleased with myself for bringing up, on the spur of the moment, such a graphic illustration.

Riley and Percy stared at the floor, Vernon at the ceiling, Ambrose and Dennis out of opposite windows. Even Agnes and Leah seemed to be looking over my shoulder at the empty blackboard. Only Raleigh looked interested.

"Well, for next week, write five sentences using possessive pronouns," I said, puzzled by their lack of response. They were usually so eager.

One evening later that week, I dropped by the Apache basket weaving class to talk with the instructor. The master weaver, Celena Perry, sat surrounded by piles of coiled cotton willow bark. She was teaching ten women, both Apache and white, how to tear with their teeth the yard-long, half-inch strips into three equal parts. I'd tried it once, and it seemed impossible to do.

When Agnes and Leah saw me come in, they cornered me in the back of the room and, their long camp dresses swishing, pushed me down into a seat between them.

"Sooonya!" said Agnes.

"We have something to tell you," said Leah.

"Yes," said Agnes, "we've been waiting to see you."

"It's a good thing you came in tonight!"

"The other night in English class..."

"You thought you were saying my brother..."

"Yes?"

"You weren't."

"I wasn't?"

"No."

"What did I say?"

They looked embarrassed.

"What did I say," I asked again.

"Well..." Agnes began.

"Well, what?"

"You said...you said..."

"I said what?"

"My penis."

I stared at them. "I said that?"

"You did."

"But I learned in my Apache class…"

"What you meant to say was *shilah*! You have to make your voice go up at the end. Up!"

"Yes! Up! Up!"

"You said '*shilaaaa*.' You made your voice go down at the end."

"My God," I said.

"And you kept saying it over and over," Agnes said.

"You just wouldn't stop." Leah giggled.

"Shilaa, shilaa, shilaaaaa…" imitated Agnes, jiggling with laughter.

"And poor Riley just stared at the floor, he felt so sorry for you," Leah said.

"And Ambrose was so *embarrassed*," Agnes said, "and Percy and Dennis…"

"And Vernon! Oh, my goodness, Vernon!"

"I noticed Raleigh was the only one who took notes," I said.

"He would," said Agnes.

Apache Tears

It was dark as we approached the Queen Creek tunnel at the entrance to Devil's Canyon that Sunday evening early in December 1973. Tired from a weekend of Christmas shopping in Phoenix and anxious to get home, Richard spun around a curve, jolting Christopher awake. Sleepily, Chris peered out the window. "Ronald's tunnel," he announced.

"Yep," said Richard. "Old Ronald built that tunnel back in 1952."

"He didn't build it all by himself," Patrick said.

"Well, no, he had help, of course," Richard said. "But, boy, does he love to tell about dynamiting the hole through that mountain."

Ronald always made me think of Apache Leap Mountain, a place we had passed a few miles back, where Apaches in the 1870s had thrown themselves to their deaths rather than surrender to the U.S. Cavalry. Apache women had wept bitter tears over their dead warriors, and those tears had turned into the small, beautiful translucent black rocks that now covered the ground at the foot of the mountain. Those rocks are called Apache Tears, and they made me think of Ronald because he was the only Apache who ever let me see him cry.

I remembered Ronald, not even fifty years old, but looking seventy, coming to our door one morning over a year ago, already drunk and very angry.

"I just think you should know, Missus, that Richard called me stupid."

"He did?"

"That's right. My friend Richard called me stupid."

"Why in the world…?"

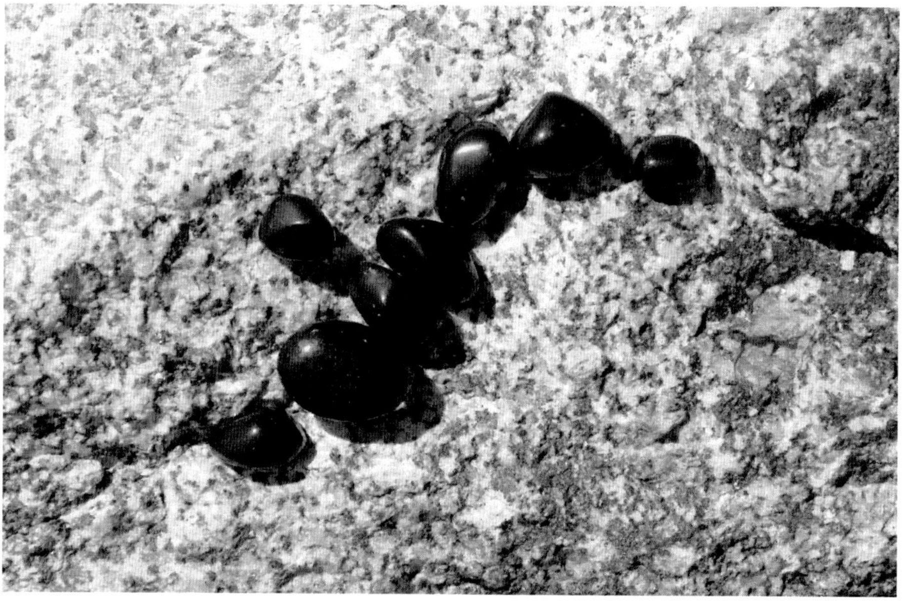

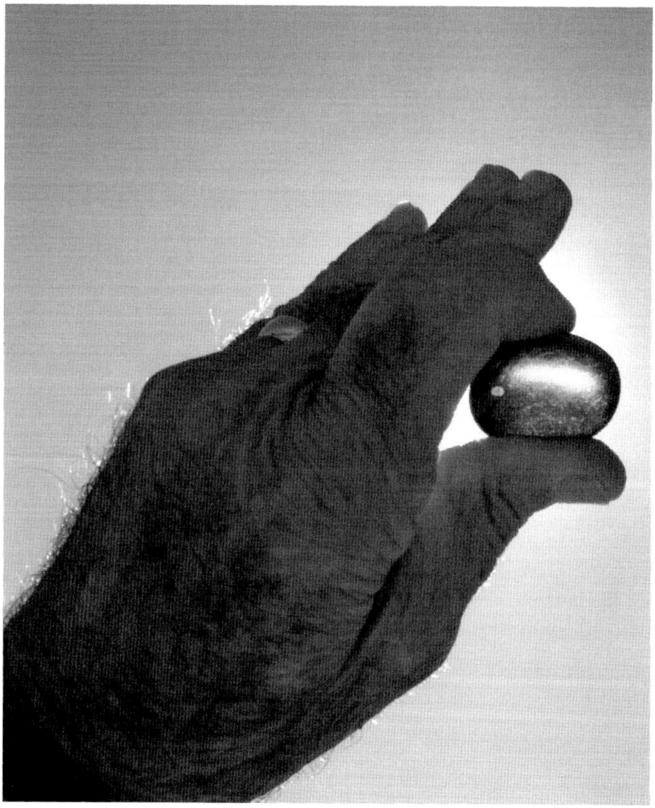

When Apache Tears are polished, they become translucent.

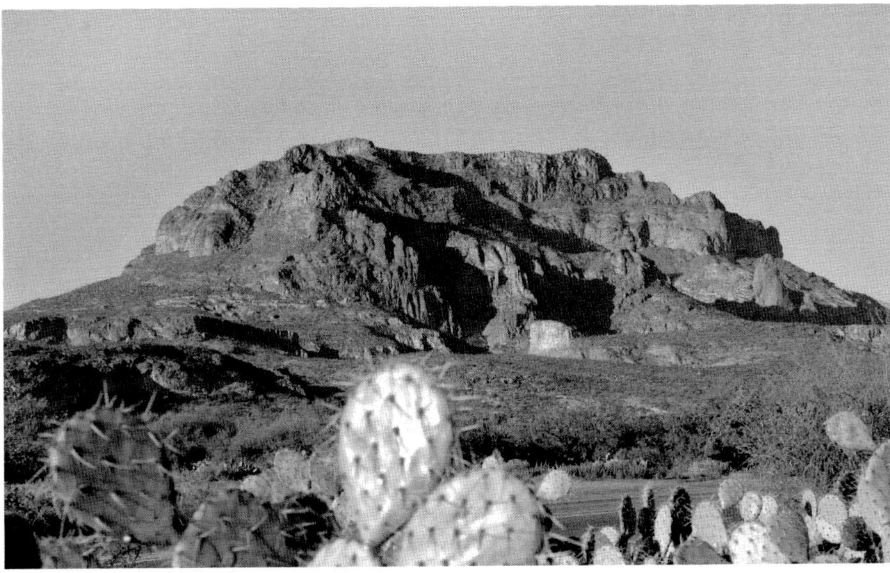

Apache Leap Mountain, where, according to legend, Apache warriors leapt to their deaths rather than surrender to the U.S. Cavalry.

"I am not stupid, and he knows that," Ronald said. A tear trickled down his cheek and into the stubby hairs on his chin.

"Oh, Lord, Ronald, what happened?"

"He hurt my feelings, Missus, and I just thought you should know." Ronald tugged on the bill of his old ball cap and walked down the sidewalk to the street.

I called Richard at the agency. "What happened between you and Ronald? He was just here and he said you called him stupid."

"I didn't say he was stupid, I said he did a stupid thing. And he did. He sold a cow for a hundred bucks to some white man in Globe and gave the money to Ronnie to buy tires."

"So you accused Ronald of letting Ronnie rip him off. Right?"

"Pretty much that," Richard said.

"You know one of these days you're going to have to quit leading Ronald around by the hand."

"He's smart, he's a good guy. It just kills me to see him drink himself to death."

"Yeah," I sighed. "But someday you'll find you can't change the world by yourself."

"Not the world," Richard said. "Just Ronald."

Richard had recently helped Ronald get both his driver's license and his Operating Engineers union membership reinstated so he could work on Arizona highway construction projects. On the way back to San Carlos from the union visit in Phoenix, Richard stopped for gas. On the pretext of going to the restroom, Ronald had headed for a bar where Richard found him half an hour later. Despairing, he hauled Ronald, proudly waving his new union card, back to the government car and home to his wife, Abbie.

Since then, Ronald had almost run me over in the parking lot of the Tribe Store. Screaming to get his attention, I grabbed Noelle and jumped to the side of his old turquoise Chevy. He waved and smiled. A few weeks later, his license once more revoked, I picked him up on the highway outside of Globe. He was so drunk he never did recognize me on the twenty-five-mile ride home.

And now, as we drove around the bend at Peridot, I automatically looked to my right at Ronald's house and saw a yellow hard hat moving toward the highway.

"Watch out for Benjamin," I cautioned, but even before I finished speaking, Richard was gearing the bus down. "Something's wrong," he said.

"What do you mean?"

"Ronald's dead."

"*What?*"

"Look over there. The bonfire, the shelters."

Peering through the dark at the land surrounding the small wooden house where Ronald and Abbie lived, I saw several temporary shades, four posts topped by a cover of cottonwood branches, which served as shelters under which food was distributed at Apache wakes.

As soon as we got home, Richard called the hospital. "What time?" I heard him say. He put down the phone. "He came home sometime this afternoon when nobody was there. Abbie found him in bed. His poor old liver finally quit." Richard looked defeated. "I guess I should be surprised it lasted as long as it did."

I thought of the Christmas morning Ronald had arrived at our house, sober and splendid in a crisp white cowboy shirt with pearl buttons and an old gray Stetson. He'd brought a small leather case containing mother-of-pearl cuff links and a tie clasp for Richard and a box of Payday candy bars for the children. "I can't imagine life around here without good old Ronald," I said.

"Neither can I," Richard said.

The next evening, Richard and I turned off the road near the Peridot Trading Post, drove the short distance to Ronald's house and parked in a line of pickup trucks and cars. We got out of the van and walked over to where a group of twenty or thirty men stood next to a bonfire. The warmth felt good in the cool winter night. Benjamin saw us and smiled.

"Good evening, Richard, Missus," he said. "Terrible, isn't it? Terrible about Ronald." He blew his nose on his fingers. "I've lost my best friend, Richard." He paused. "By the way, you got fifty cents?"

Richard felt in his pocket, found two quarters and handed them to Benjamin.

"I think we should go see Abbie," I said.

The door frame of Ronald's house—even some of the boards beyond the frame—had been removed to allow Ronald's casket to be brought in. The tiny living room was full of people and large bouquets of flowers: salmon-colored gladioli, white carnations, red and pink roses. A powder blue lace mantilla floated down from the raised lid of the casket and over Ronald's face. I had never seen that done before, and I wondered why it was there. A black rosary had been woven through his fingers. I doubted if Ronald had ever prayed the rosary in his life. Had Abbie placed the beads in her husband's hands? Perhaps she had. Perhaps she had put them there as a way of showing respect to Father Bart for stepping up to bury Ronald when her own minister, calling Ronald an old pagan, declined the honor.

Abbie, wearing a traditional long, flowered camp dress, came over to us and put her arms around Richard. She began to cry. He embraced her and bent his head on top of hers.

"I want you to say Ronald's eulogy, Richard," she said. "You were his best friend. Say something good."

"I will, Abbie," he promised.

"Ronald was an intelligent man," Richard said in the Catholic mission a week later. "I can still see him walking around with a *Newsweek* magazine rolled up in his back pocket. He said he had to keep up with national news and politics. He got me to agree with him on many issues. Did I try to make Ronald into a white man? I don't know, but I do know he made me into an Indian. He used to tell me that. 'I'm turning you into an Apache,' he would say. I know a lot of white people thought it was weird, but he caught me up in his family.

"Ronald was a good Apache. He prayed every morning at dawn. He would say, 'I may be drunk by noon but every morning when the sun rises I face the mountains and I pray.'

"'Who do you pray for, Ronald?' I asked him.

"'For me, for my wife, for my children, for the Apaches, for you, too,' he said.

"I believe Ronald is there now." Richard pointed in the direction of the mountain called the Triplets behind the church. "I think he prays for us. I hope so."

Richard turned from the pulpit. He stopped and looked down at the coffin. "One more thing," he said. "Ronald and I once had a terrible argument. It was after he sold a cow to buy tires for one of his boys. 'Why do you always let them take advantage of you?' I shouted. Ronald looked at me like I was crazy. 'Because they're my sons,' he said."

Richard looked out over the congregation. "I've discovered Ronald was right. He knew what was important."

Abbie, in the front pew, smiled.

We stood in the dirt yard in front of the church, the two palm trees towering over the roof, as Ronald's sons carried his coffin out into the sunlight. Behind them marched Benjamin, still wearing his yellow hard hat, bearing the American flag.

CHILIBOY

"You are not paying attention! In fact, you *never* pay attention!"

Sister Conquistadora's high, shrill voice grated like fingernails on a blackboard. *Crack*! My shoulders jerked as she stamped one small, tightly laced foot on the wooden podium.

"You seem determined not to sing correctly!"

The ninety-six children (the entire student body of St. Charles School, minus one) stood stiffly on the risers in front of her, their faces, for the most part, impassive and Apache but lightened here and there by a rebellious patch of white. Christopher, my first grader, turned up his fat, round face and stuck out his tongue—she didn't see!—and Patrick poked his buddies in the ribs, Douglas on one side and Terrel on the other.

"She hates all three of us," Patrick had told me earlier.

"Oh, she doesn't hate you!" I'd protested.

"Oh, yes she does!" Doug had assured me. "It just kills her that me and Pat get the highest grades in her class because she hates boys even worse than she hates Apaches. Right, Terrel?" The one dark-skinned member of the trio, damned apparently on both counts, had nodded stoically.

"If you do not get it right, I will *not* let you sing in the program!" Sister Conquistadora cried, motioning for Sister Mary to shift the portable record player needle onto the guitar recording.

"Now this time pay attention to my hands! *My hands*!"

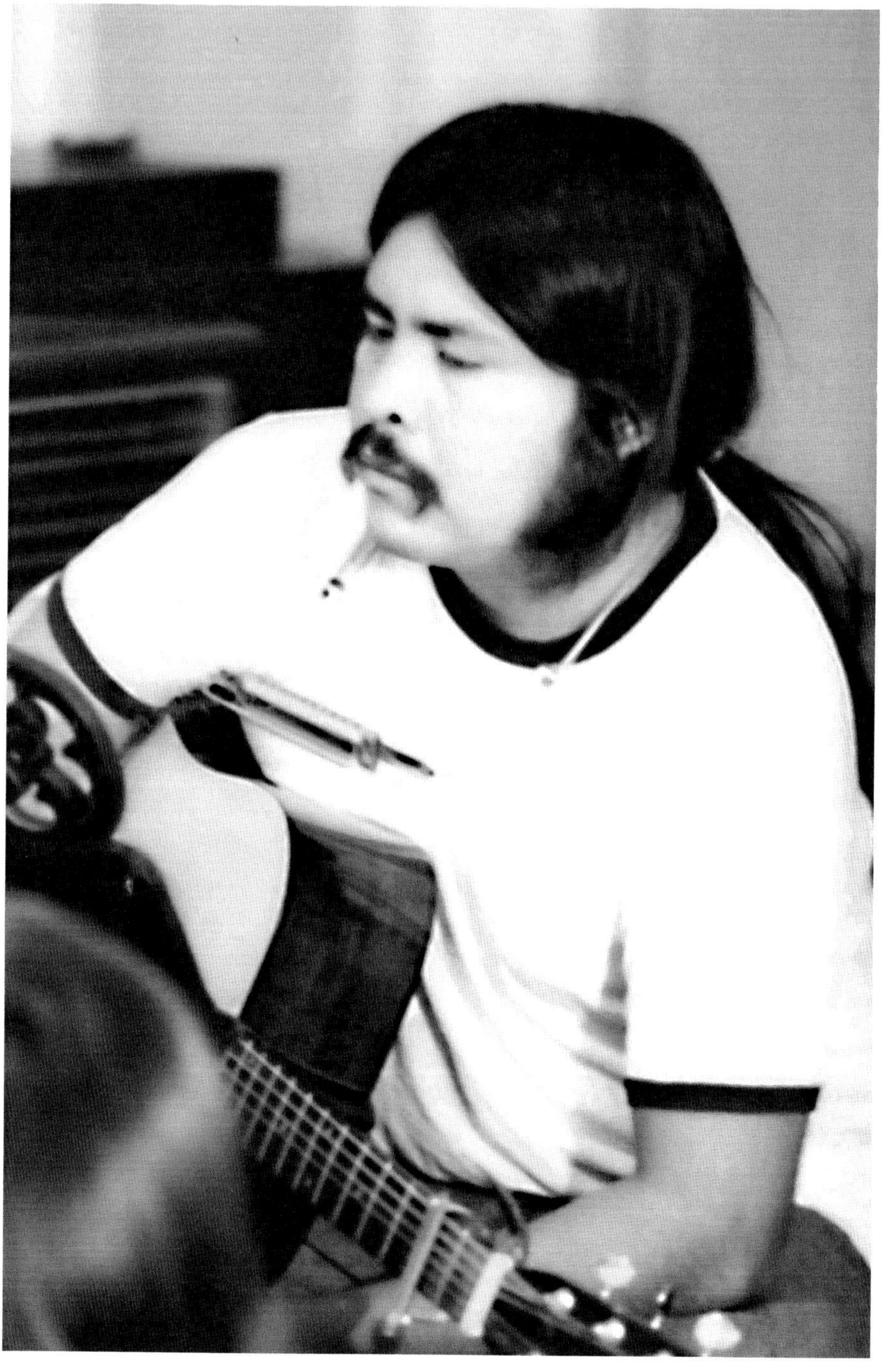

Chiliboy.

As she waved one hand in the air, trying to get the children to start singing along with the record, she pointed with the other at Doug's mother, Nancy Schmidt, to begin the piano accompaniment.

"What a disaster!" Nancy whispered to me. "I mean, she sings sharp and she can't keep time! How do you follow her in church?"

"We don't," I muttered. "Nobody sings." Nobody, in fact, had sung since Sister Conquistadora, replacing Sister Consolata who'd been transferred to another mission, insisted upon assuming (with a distinctly martyred air) Consolata's extracurricular role of church musician.

Next to the piano an almond-eyed elf banged on a triangle. When Conquistadora banished five-year-old clown Bart Stevens from the choir, Nancy had protested.

"I don't think that's fair…or wise," she'd cautioned Sister Conquistadora. "Bart's mother has been looking forward to his first school program for weeks."

"These children *will* know who is in charge, Mrs. Schmidt!"

"He can sit with me, then," Nancy said, smoldering. "He can play the triangle."

Sister Conquistadora, elbows bent, fists clenched, stood at sharp angles to everyone around her. Gaunt as an El Greco figure in her navy veil and dress, her mouth and eyebrows were slashed in horizontal lines across an unmistakably Spanish face.

"Santa Fe Spanish, *not* Mexican," she would quickly correct anyone ignorant enough to make that mistake.

And woe unto the person who mistook her for an Indian!

"*My* people brought civilization to the Pueblo Indians!" she would say. "And I am proud to be carrying on that tradition among the Apaches. The wild Apaches. Even the Pueblos look down on them! But like my ancestors, my passion is for their immortal souls."

Your ancestors' passion was for Apache slaves, I would retort, silently, wondering how long I could keep my mouth shut around this sister who'd taken her name in religion after the statue of the Virgin that the Conquistadors brought with them into New Spain. La Conquistadora, the Lady Conqueror of the Indians.

I cringed, embarrassed, whenever, at Mass, we sang the line in *America, the Beautiful* about "pilgrim feet, whose stern impassioned stress/ A thoroughfare of freedom beat across the wilderness."

It certainly hadn't turned out to be a "thoroughfare of freedom" for the Indians, I would think as I'd glance, surreptitiously, at the people around me and wonder if they were secretly offended by the words that Conquistadora's thin, reedy voice flung out across the mute congregation.

I'd once actually asked Sister Conquistadora if we could skip over the second verse.

"Of course not," she'd replied, scowling at me. "That verse glorifies God. And we are here for no other reason than to glorify God." How did reminding the Indians of their defeat glorify God?

"Because in their defeat they found *salvation*!" she'd hissed.

Up until now, I'd loved the sisters at the mission school. They'd taught my sons gently and well. But this new sister, this conqueror from Santa Fe, was a throwback to a meaner time, before Pope John XXIII "opened the windows" of the church. For this particular sister, windows did not exist.

One morning the previous fall when I was in Globe, Sister Anne Regina, the principal, called Richard at work to tell him that Patrick had disappeared from Sister Conquistadora's third-grade classroom. Richard rushed home and found Patrick hiding behind the juniper tree in the front yard.

"I'm not going back," Patrick announced, his face curled into a scowl. "*Never*."

"Please, Patrick," coaxed Sister Anne Regina, who arrived at our house soon after Richard.

"No."

"But you love school," she reminded him. She'd been his first-grade teacher and had taught him how to read.

"Not anymore."

"Oh, come on, Patrick boy," begged Patrice, the little Irish nun who had, by this time, walked over from the schoolyard to see what was going on.

"I'll go back to you but not to *her*!"

"But we can't put you all the way back in second grade!" Patrice exclaimed, trying to make a joke of it.

"Please, Patrick," Anne Regina pleaded. "For my sake?"

"And for me?" Patrice chirped.

For those two, of course, he'd do anything, even return to Sister Conquistadora. But the remainder of the year throbbed with tension, and I was relieved that only a week of school remained.

"You are all *stupid*!" Sister Conquistadora screeched, cracking her shoe once more on the podium. "Stupid! Stupid—"

"Look, maybe I can help," I blurted out, scarcely aware of what I said as I jumped up.

"*You*, Mrs. David?" Sister Conquistadora turned and glared at me.

"Yes," I said, my heart pounding with anger.

"*You*, Mrs. David?" Sister Conquistadora repeated, one eyebrow popping up. "What can *you* do?"

"Well, I could lead the singing!"

"Oh, you could, could you?"

"Yes, I could!" I lied, glaring back at her.

Sister Conquistadora's eyes narrowed and her nostrils flared.

The palms of my hands began to sweat as I realized what I'd done. *Fools rush in*, I thought, half fearing she'd accept my foolish offer.

"Fine," hissed Conquistadora. "*You* lead the singing, Mrs. David. It's all *yours*." She swept off the podium. As she stomped toward the door of the parish hall, Sister Patrice fluttered after her, clucking and cajoling, but Conquistadora pushed her aside. Sister Anne Regina's mouth twitched. Then she shrugged her shoulders and nodded her head in my direction.

I stepped tentatively up on the podium and looked at the children. I'd never led anything musical in my life. Although I'd played flute years before in the Phoenix Youth Symphony, when it came to singing I could barely squeak. Richard should be doing this, I thought, with his fine, strong baritone. But Richard wasn't here and I was. And hadn't I sat through years and years of my mother's church choir rehearsals as a child, observing each distinct and separate movement of her hands? I took a deep breath, lifted my own hands and began.

After the rehearsal, Nancy and I decided to chuck the scratchy record in favor of the real thing.

"Can't you play your guitar?" she asked, referring to the one she'd seen hanging on the wall of our living room.

"That's a relic of my hippie days," I joked. "A lost cause. Believe me. When it comes to guitar playing, I'm right up there with Sister Conquistadora."

Nancy laughed and then suggested an Apache named Sluggo, who worked as a disc jockey.

"The guy on crutches?" I asked. "And all that curly hair? I've seen him in church. I think he's a Catholic."

"Well, then he can't turn us down, can he?" Nancy said, determined. "We'll make him feel guilty if he does!"

We found Sluggo leaning on his crutches (he had been crippled since childhood from polio) and spinning records in a narrow room behind the forestry office. The room had been converted into use for the low-frequency radio station, which was unlicensed and limited to the reservation.

"This is an old one from…the *'60s*!" Sluggo announced into the microphone as he flipped a Beatles record onto the turntable.

"What's up?" he asked, switching off the mike.

"Sure," he said, after we explained the reason for our visit. "I'll play for the program, if you can drive me over to the school."

"Oh, yes!" I assured him, elated. "Where do you live?"

"With the Machukays. You know where that is?" I nodded, wondering how many more people, in addition to her own family, the saintly Martha could cram into her tiny house behind the hospital compound.

When I drove the VW van over to Martha's two days later, she came out to greet me, her battered tennis shoes kicking the hem of her long camp dress, her old face wrinkled into that sweet smile.

"Hi, Martha," I said, hopping down from the van. "I've come to drive Sluggo to the school. Is he here?"

"Well, yes, I guess maybe so." Martha hesitated for a second, caught her breath and then chuckled in her low, gentle voice.

"Is he ready?" I asked. "The rehearsal starts in about ten minutes."

"Yes, OK, I'll tell him that," she said as she turned back toward the house. "I'll tell him you said that."

Five minutes later, I checked my watch impatiently. Where in the world was he? He'd better hurry if we weren't going to be late! I was about ready to go in after him when suddenly, Martha's front door banged open and Sluggo, carrying a guitar case, lurched on his crutches across the dirt yard. Relieved, I opened the van door and slid it back.

"You had me worried," I said as he handed me the guitar case. I was placing it carefully on the floor of the van when, behind me, I heard him mutter, "I can't."

"You *what*?" I spun around.

"I can't play for you."

"Why not?" I noticed for the first time the fine layer of sweat covering his face. He looked, for an Indian, abnormally pale. "Are you sick?" I asked.

"Well, sort of," he said.

"What do you mean?"

"I've got a hangover."

"A *hangover*! Sluggo…"

"I *can't*!"

"Oh, but you *must*!" I cried, thinking of the children and the sisters waiting for us over at the school. Especially the sisters. Especially Sister Conquistadora. I thought about how Nancy and I had bragged about our live guitar player, and I could just see Conquistadora's smug smile when I arrived without him.

"You *promised*!" I wailed, wondering why he'd bothered to bring out his guitar. What good was a guitar without someone to play it? "Sluggo, you promised me! What about the program? What about the children? The sisters?"

"Shhh," he said, suddenly staring down at the ground. "Don't yell."

"Couldn't you give it a try?" I begged. "Please…"

"Don't worry," Sluggo said, holding up his hand for me to be quiet.

"Don't *worry*?" I could already see Sister Conquistadora's smug smile turning to a sneer.

"That's right," Sluggo said, closing his eyes. He swayed for a moment on his crutches and then brushed one hand across his forehead. "Don't worry. I got you Chiliboy."

"You got me what?"

"Chiliboy."

As if on cue, a handsome young guy strode out of Martha's house and over toward the van. He had a handlebar mustache (unusual in Apaches) and the longest hair I'd ever seen on a man. It floated far over his shoulders and down to his waist like a Bedouin tent.

"Who's that?" I whispered to Sluggo.

"Chiliboy," Sluggo said.

"Chiliboy," I repeated after him, wondering if anyone could really be named that. "Can he play the guitar?"

"Oh, boy!" Sluggo looked at me as if I were out of my mind. "Can he play the *guitar*!"

And Sluggo was right. Chiliboy could play the guitar. He couldn't read music, but he didn't have to. Whatever Nancy played on the piano, whatever the children sang, in whatever key, Chiliboy followed along, improvising harmonies, sometimes coming out and taking the lead with the melody. In perfect, absolutely perfect, time.

Nancy and I exchanged exhilarated glances.

As I led the singing, I mouthed the words to the songs and flung my arms around in a flamboyant imitation of my mother.

"Isn't it lovely?" Sister Patrice said, smiling happily.

Sister Anne Regina's mouth twitched.

Sister Conquistadora glared.

Bart pounded the triangle.

The children trilled like a bunch of meadowlarks.

And Chiliboy sat there on a rusty folding chair next to the old, upright piano, his fingers flashing across the strings of Sluggo's guitar, smiling cheerily.

ONE DAY IN LATE June, the old Mexican bell on the front porch rang once, then paused and rang again.

"Nice day, isn't it?" Chiliboy said when I opened the door. He wore aviator sunglasses.

"A hundred and five degrees is nice?" I countered, surprised to see him for the first time since the night of the school program a month before. "In Phoenix it's a hundred and ten in the shade, so I guess we're lucky!"

He laughed.

"Would you like to come in, Chiliboy?" I asked, knowing, of course, he'd say no. I realized we hadn't been acquainted long enough or well enough for him to enter our house. Whatever business he had would be transacted right here on the front porch.

"Yup," he replied, surprising me for the second time.

"Well, uh, how about some iced tea?" I asked, thrown off balance as he followed me boldly into the living room.

"Sure," he said.

I escaped to the kitchen, wondering what in the world he wanted. When I returned with the tea he accepted it silently, and we stood there, not speaking, for several awkward minutes.

"Nice guitar you got there," he finally said, gazing at the wall above the piano.

"Well, here, try it out," I told him, relieved to have something to talk about. I lifted the guitar down from the wall and handed it to him.

Is this what he'd come for? To play my guitar? But why would he do that? Didn't he have one of his own? Of course, he'd played Sluggo's guitar for the school program, but I hadn't thought much about that, since he'd filled in for Sluggo at the last minute.

"This come from Chicago?" Chiliboy asked, running his fingers over the delicate inlay of the highly varnished wood.

"From Spain," I told him.

"You play it?"

"No," I said.

"Why not?"

"I took a few guitar lessons but finally admitted it wasn't my thing. Especially when I got pregnant and couldn't hold the guitar on my lap anymore."

He laughed.

"Go ahead, play it," I urged him, again.

"OK," he said, pulling out a bentwood chair to sit on. He tuned the guitar, strummed a few quick chords and then began to pick a bright flamenco. His fingers moved so rapidly they blurred, and the notes sparkled, clear and resonant.

I caught my breath. "You really *are* good!" I said, stunned by his technique, which went far beyond the simple religious folk songs he'd played for the children's program.

He laughed again, his eyes narrowing into slits, as he slowed into a fandango.

"Where did you learn to play like that?" I asked him.

"From my daddy," he said, picking the strings at random. "In the bootleggers' camp."

He learned that in a bootleggers' camp?

"This guitar's kind of quiet," he said.

"Quiet?"

"I can't make it sound very loud."

"Well, I guess you're used to steel guitars."

He nodded.

"But classical guitars are more subtle," I told him. "And I think it sounds good in here, with the wooden floors and high ceilings. Especially when *you* play it."

"Yeah, it does sound real good in here, even the soft notes," he agreed, changing from Mexican to jazz.

He played for an hour, and then he abruptly stood up and handed the guitar back to me.

"Thanks for the concert," I said. "Come back and play again."

"Sure." He laughed. "Sometime."

I wondered if he meant it.

He did. He began dropping by often, especially in the evenings, when he and Richard would sing together. They made an engaging duet, with Richard's strong baritone and Chiliboy's Louis Armstrong rasp. But curiously, instead of the instrument accompanying the singing, it seemed to me their voices provided the background for the extraordinary music Chiliboy created.

In addition to his own concoctions, he introduced us to two songs by an American Indian folk singer that were apparently popular at the time among Native Americans. One lampooned anthropologists who came out to the reservation to study "their fine feathered friends," and the other, more caustic, criticized Christian missionaries for meddling with the souls of Indians. We found ourselves squirming and laughing, simultaneously.

We discovered, to our amazement, that Chiliboy did not own a guitar. The fact that he'd learned to play the way he did on borrowed instruments, and without a teacher, seemed nearly miraculous. Several nights a week we'd hear the Mexican bell ring, and there would be Chiliboy on our front porch.

"Nice day, isn't it?" he'd always say, regardless of what time it was, as I handed him my guitar.

One evening when the Mexican bell rang, a young, pregnant girl, her dark hair pulled back from her thin, pretty face, stood next to Chiliboy.

"This is Carolyn," he said.

"Come in, guys! Come on in," Richard said. "Nice to meet you, Carolyn."

Carolyn sat quietly on the couch and listened intently to the music. Occasionally, she would smile, but she rarely said a word. And from then on, whenever Chiliboy came to our house, Carolyn was with him.

"How would you like to sing in church?" Richard asked Chiliboy one night.

"Sing in *church*?" Chiliboy said, sounding astonished. "*Me*?"

"Sure, why not?" Richard grinned mischievously.

"But what about, uh, old Sister what's her name?" Chiliboy asked, obviously remembering Conquistadora's glaring face from the night he'd played at the school program.

"She's gone for the summer," Richard told him. "All the sisters are. They won't be back until school starts in the fall."

"Me? Play in church?" Chiliboy repeated. But he looked pleased at the idea.

"I bet Father Bart wouldn't mind letting us do some music," Richard said. "Just until the sisters get back, of course," he added.

"Of course," I said, already seeing the plan form inside my husband's head. "You're so transparent," I teased him.

"Who, *me*?" Richard protested innocently.

"Well, why not?" Father Bart said when Richard approached him with the

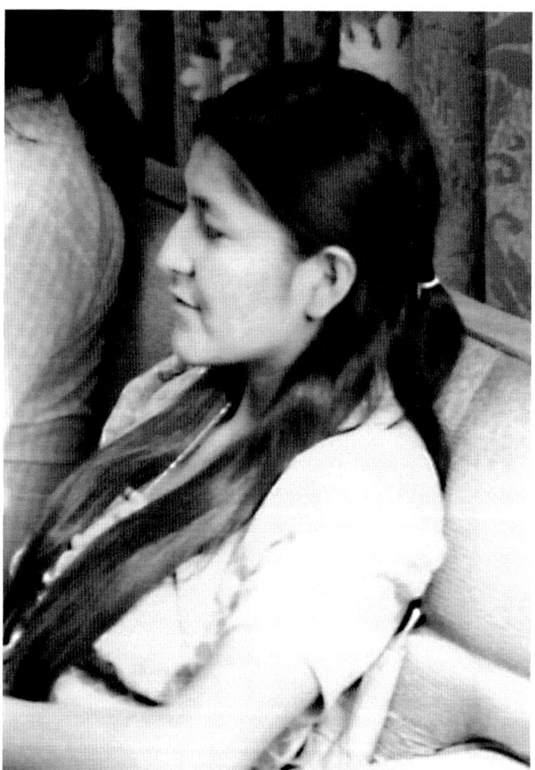

Chiliboy's wife, Carolyn.

idea. "That would be fine! Just until the sisters return, of course." I recalled Conquistadora at the front of the church, playing the wheezy organ, off-key, off-beat.

On Saturday night, Richard and Chiliboy took our stereo speakers and amplifier along with a microphone over to the mission and worked for hours creating a sound system in the little church. By Sunday morning they were ready, and as people trooped in for Mass, Chiliboy, sitting up by the altar rail, strummed softly on the guitar while Richard distributed mimeographed song sheets with words to some of the songs from the musical *Godspell*.

At first Richard was singing by himself, but gradually his strong voice drew a few others in, and by the time we got to the recessional, "Prepare Ye the Way of the Lord," half the congregation was singing, which was something of a record for St. Charles Mission.

"That was real good," Louise Ward told them after Mass. "You guys gonna do that again next week?"

"Hey, Richard, do you know 'Hear, Oh, Lord, the Sound of My Call'?" Agnes Houzous asked. "That's my favorite."

"Our first request!" Richard said, elated.

By the end of the summer, Richard and Chiliboy were packing them in on Sunday mornings. Father Bart had to put folding chairs down one side of the aisle. People who hadn't been to Mass in years, or who'd shown up at Easter and Christmas, began to appear week after week.

One Sunday, I was surprised to see Agnes's son, David, the pallbearer in the Edwardian frock coat with whom I had been so captivated at the first funeral I attended in San Carlos, sitting with three of his friends in the front row.

"David comes to Mass because he likes the music," Agnes told me, apparently as surprised as I was to see her son in church. "What do you think about that? They're pretty good, that Richard and Chiliboy!"

"Isn't it *lovely*?" Sister Patrice exclaimed as she looked over the crowd her first Sunday back from Philadelphia. "The people are suddenly responding so well to Father's wonderful sermons!"

Sister Anne Regina's eyes twinkled, but Sister Conquistadora, her mouth tight, refused to look at Richard and Chiliboy.

Father Bart mentioned that perhaps Sister Conquistadora might do the music again, but Richard and I argued with him, and he gave in.

One Wednesday evening, Sister Mary Delorey brought some of the schoolchildren to the Teacherage "to learn the music and help out with the congregational singing." I passed around cookies and punch, and the St. Charles Mission choir was born.

"That looks like the Republican National Committee in there," Chiliboy said, coming to a sudden halt and peering through the doorway into the crowded social hall of the Mormon church in Globe.

Republican National Committee? Richard and I glanced at each other behind Chiliboy's back and smiled.

"Well, let's get on in there and sing," Richard said, prodding Chiliboy forward.

"In front of all those people?" Chiliboy asked, hesitantly.

"Sure, why not?" Richard said. "We do this every Sunday in San Carlos."

"Not in a gymnasium," Chiliboy retorted. "You didn't tell me this was gonna be in a *gymnasium*!"

"Oh, what difference does it make?" Richard asked.

Chiliboy looked at Richard as if he were crazy.

When our children's piano teacher, Bessie Park, called Richard to ask him and Chiliboy to provide some music for her daughter's reception the week after their Salt Lake City Temple wedding, she'd told him to sing whatever they wanted.

"Just anything," she'd said when he'd tried to pin her down. "Just whatever you usually do."

"We'll do fine," Richard now assured Chiliboy as he shoved him inside the door and propelled him toward the stage at the end of the hall.

My friend Joyce Montgomery from Peridot Trading Post waved at me from somewhere in the middle of the room, and Carolyn and I made our way over to where she was sitting.

"I think this is real nice that Richard and Chiliboy are singing here tonight," Joyce said to us as we sat down next to her.

"Boy, wait 'til you hear these guys," I heard her tell someone on her left as she settled back comfortably in her chair. "They're just terrific! You should come out and hear 'em sometime at the Catholic church in San Carlos."

"Where are the bride and groom?" I asked.

Joyce motioned toward a row of seats near the stage where the newlyweds, both swathed from head to foot in pure white, sat in a place of honor.

I began to have misgivings as I watched beehived women wearing tulle "formals" and shorthaired men in pastel suits ascend the stairs, face the audience and croon old Broadway show tunes. On and on they came, in singles and groups, one act following the other in a flawless display of '50s gentility.

And then I saw Richard nudge Chiliboy (his hair falling over his face) to the center of the stage. In their white lace Mexican wedding shirts, they looked like hippies.

Chiliboy sat down, whipped out his dark glasses and put them on. He stared straight ahead.

"The bride and groom thought it would be nice to have some of the folks from San Carlos take part in this reception tonight," the master of ceremonies announced. "This is Mr. David and Mr...Chiliboy?"

He looked, uncertainly, at the piece of paper in his hand.

"Well, they're from San Carlos," he finished feebly and coughed. "Neighbors of the bride."

The audience clapped politely.

"Just wait 'til you hear these guys!" Joyce's loud whisper carried across the room.

I saw Chiliboy strum the guitar. I saw his mouth move. And Richard's. They looked like mimes. Chiliboy had been right. As soon as he'd seen where they had to play, he had known what would happen. Even with the microphone, the muted tones from the nylon strings of my classical guitar were lost in this cavernous gymnasium.

The audience rustled.

"Can't hear you!" someone called out.

Chiliboy's hand froze.

"Could you sing a little louder, please?" The master of ceremonies pleaded.

Suddenly, Richard flung out his arms and threw back his head.

"We come to feast at the table of love!" he belted out in a syrupy vibrato. He strolled across the stage and winked down at the bride and groom.

I slunk down in my seat.

"Oh, yes...oh yes..." he warbled relentlessly, turning the Catholic communion hymn into a pop tune. "The table of...LOVE!"

Chiliboy, behind his dark glasses, sat like a rock.

"I can't understand it," I heard Joyce whisper. "They're usually just terrific."

"My God," Richard muttered after we'd escaped. "My God. I didn't know we were going to be on a *stage*!"

"You never went to a Mormon wedding reception before?" I asked him, surprised. "What did you expect?"

"People walking around, talking, eating little chicken sandwiches and stuff while we did some background music. *You* know."

"They're always like that. They're regular shows," I said.

"Why didn't you warn me?" he asked.

"I thought you knew," I said. "I mean, we grew up in the same town. I can't believe you never went to a Mormon wedding reception!"

"Was I really bad?" Richard asked. "Did I embarrass everybody? I decided I'd better do *something*."

"No," I said. "You sounded just like Perry Como."

"Perry Como!" Chiliboy howled from the back of the van. "Perry Como at the table of LOVE!"

That Christmas Eve, before Midnight Mass, Chiliboy, Carolyn and their baby girl, Lynnia, arrived with a gift for Richard: a silver medallion on a silver chain. The medallion, over two inches in diameter, was a replica of an Indian Head nickel but with the profile of the Indian on both sides. At the top was the word "Liberty," and by the best of coincidences, the nickel was dated 1937, the year of Richard's birth. I had never seen another one like it. Who knows where Chiliboy found it? He certainly did not know when Richard was born. That Indian Head medallion became one of Richard's most treasured possessions.

In late May 1974, Father Bart arrived at our house to tell us that David Houzous, Agnes's son, had been killed in a car accident in Phoenix. He had been only twenty-two years old. David Houzous, my young Geronimo.

Agnes wanted the congregation to sing her favorite song, "Hear, Oh, Lord, the Sound of My Cry." Chiliboy played that, of course, along with several others. David's funeral Mass was one of the saddest I had ever witnessed. After David's coffin was carried from the church and most of the people had gone, I saw Chiliboy step through the door. Richard called to him, but he seemed not to hear. He ran down the street away from us, his wondrous hair flying out behind him. I think he did not want us to see his tears.

How could we know we would not see Chiliboy again until forty years later, during a monsoon August when the rain, so rare in Arizona, was pouring down and flooding much of the reservation? When he heard we were in San Carlos, he called us on his cellphone and told us exactly where to meet him. We saw his pickup truck tear across the floodwaters running over Tulapai Avenue and screech to a stop. We heard him call our names as we ran toward him. We saw that his hair was now gray and cut very short. He embraced us, and he did not seem to mind that we saw his tears. When he took our hands in his and said a prayer of thanksgiving for the return of his old friends, I understood for the first time the meaning of heaven.

Eagle Feathers

What are you humming?" I asked Ambrose and Raleigh, who were sitting in the front row of my English class. It was an evening in early December, and the semester was nearly at an end.

"We are not humming," Raleigh corrected me. "We are *singing*."

"*You* are singing," Ambrose corrected Raleigh. "I am *trying* to sing."

"Well, then, what are you *trying* to sing?"

"Apache songs," Ambrose said. "Holy songs."

"But Ambrose doesn't know how," Raleigh said, "so I am teaching him."

"Why don't you know how?" I asked.

"Nobody ever taught me," Ambrose said. "But I am not doing very good," he admitted. "It's too hard."

On Christmas Eve, when Chiliboy was at our house practicing the music with Richard for the Midnight Mass, Linda came to tell us that Ambrose was drinking. Ambrose was an alcoholic, but he was sober most of the time. I had never seen him drunk. He drank in binges, and because his liver was nearly destroyed, he knew every binge might be his last. Linda asked Richard if he would please go after Ambrose and bring him home. Richard found him at a party. Although Richard persuaded Ambrose to come out to the front porch, he refused to go any farther.

"Come on, Ambrose," Richard said. "Let's go. It's freezing. You'll make me catch pneumonia."

"Me, too," Ambrose said. He would not budge.

"OK, Ambrose." Richard took off his jacket. "I will get pneumonia."

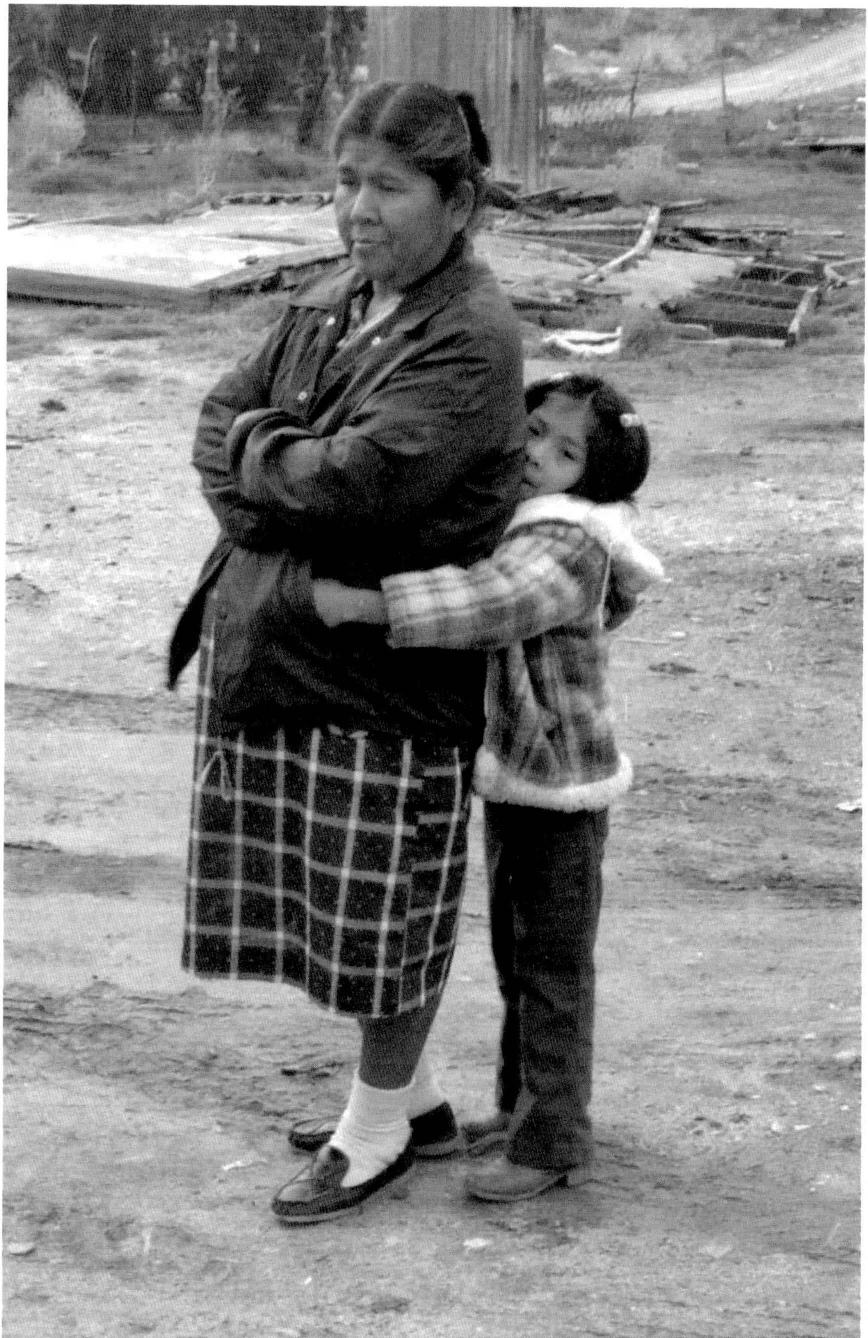

Linda Hoffman, one of my closest friends on the San Carlos Reservation, is shown here with her granddaughter.

Ambrose took off his jacket.

Richard took off his shirt. "If I get pneumonia maybe I will die."

Ambrose took off his shirt.

"If I die it will be your fault." Richard took off his undershirt, and so did Ambrose. They stood there, half naked, gritting their teeth, staring at each other, shivering.

"If you get me cigarettes I will come home," Ambrose said.

One afternoon, late, Dr. Kryc called Richard at the agency to tell him that Ambrose had been found by the river, unconscious and hemorrhaging, and that he had been taken down to Phoenix Indian Hospital in the small aircraft the Indian Health Service kept at Sky Harbor Airport for emergencies.

"He can't last through the night," Richard told me on the telephone. "That's what Joe Kryc said. Ambrose will not make it." Richard's voice broke. "He will die before morning."

I hung up the phone. I stood by the kitchen door and looked out into the dining room at the folk art Holy Spirit dove in its burst of gold rays hanging above the window. When Richard and I found the wooden dove in Puebla, Mexico, it was broken in half and held together with baling wire. It had once hung from the ceiling of a Mexican church.

"Just Mexican primitive," the antiques dealer had scoffed. "Only a hundred years old. You can have it for eight American dollars." We brought the dove home on the train, and Richard repaired it.

I was aware of the Mexican dove, of the western sun streaming in, golden on the white walls, infusing my house and the air around me with warmth and light, aware of the juniper tree outside the window, the mesquite tree and the prickly pear cactus in the driveway, of the sky, the earth, of Ambrose one hundred miles away.

Let Ambrose live, I prayed to the dove. *Make him whole. Do not let him die. Make him live.*

After Ambrose recovered, Richard and I drove to Ambrose and Linda's house. Although they had been to our house many times, we had never been to theirs. Apaches, like Navajos, do not often welcome white people into their homes. But that evening they invited us, for the first time ever, to come inside. Their home was one room: it had a dirt floor, a bed and not much else. It seemed emptier than a wickiup.

Ambrose looked wonderful, healthy. Not like a man who had nearly died a couple of weeks earlier. He told us what had happened.

"They thought I was unconscious," Ambrose said, "but I think I was just asleep because an old, old medicine man came to visit me."

"You mean he came to visit you in a dream?" I asked.

"I don't know. Maybe a dream. Maybe not a dream. But this medicine man was *there*."

"Did he sing for you?"

"That old medicine man taught *me* how to sing," Ambrose said. "He made me sing along with him. We sang for a long, long time. He made me sing until I got it *right*!" He laughed. "I finally learned how to sing."

A few days later, Linda walked up our sidewalk. She carried two eagle feathers. Since living among the Apaches, I had often thought the bald eagle, with its attributes of wisdom and power, was a stronger symbol than the dove for the Spirit of God. I longed to possess eagle feathers, but I knew that was not possible. Only Native Americans are allowed, and only for ceremonial religious purposes, to own feathers of the endangered eagle.

"These eagle feathers are very old," Linda told me. She put the feathers into my hand. "A very old medicine woman gave them to me before she died. She was almost a hundred years old."

"I've never even touched an eagle feather," I said. "They're wonderful." And they were: dark gray fading to brown and finally to white, I thought they must look as beautiful as the day, perhaps a half century before, they'd been taken from the eagle.

"I want to give these feathers to you."

"Oh, I can't, I can't," I said, wanting them with all my heart. "You *know* I can't!

"For you," she repeated.

"But the federal law…"

"Nobody will know," Linda said. She giggled, turned around and walked away. Linda was poor, she possessed so little, but she had given me her greatest treasure—the most perfect gift I had ever received.

I took the eagle feathers into the house and placed them in the golden rays of the Mexican dove.

We would stay in San Carlos, I decided. We would not be like other white people and move away. We would have another child, a baby to be born and raised here in this community of Apaches. We might even stay here for the rest of our lives. I had never belonged anywhere as I belonged here.

My House of Light

The late afternoon November sun shone gently through the juniper trees and into the tall, deep windows of my house. I loved the light of Arizona autumn, as gold as Spanish sherry, reflecting off the whitewashed walls. On days such as these I drifted, dreamlike, beneath the high ceilings with the old cast-iron chandeliers, imagining I lived a century ago.

I had fought for this house. When we first moved to San Carlos, we'd lived in an ordinary modern stucco box, identical to government quarters on every reservation from Pine Ridge, South Dakota, to Shiprock, New Mexico, and I would look longingly at the big, old houses with their wonderful, wide porches and thick walls made from square chunks of yellow-brown tufa stone that had been quarried right here on the reservation.

The house next to the Catholic mission was different from the other stone houses. Instead of a front porch, it was surrounded on three sides by a wide, covered veranda, and its steeply slanted roof was crowned by a cupola. An ancient juniper tree to the west and a row of tall salt cedars to the south created a sheltered ambience I found most inviting. The day I heard the occupants of that house were to be transferred to another reservation, I asked the BIA superintendent if he would assign it to our family.

"That old wreck?" he said. "I thought I'd tear it down!"

"*Tear it down?*"

"It needs too much work," he said. "These old houses all do. It's cheaper to build new ones."

"But they're worth preserving!" I protested. "They're historic!"

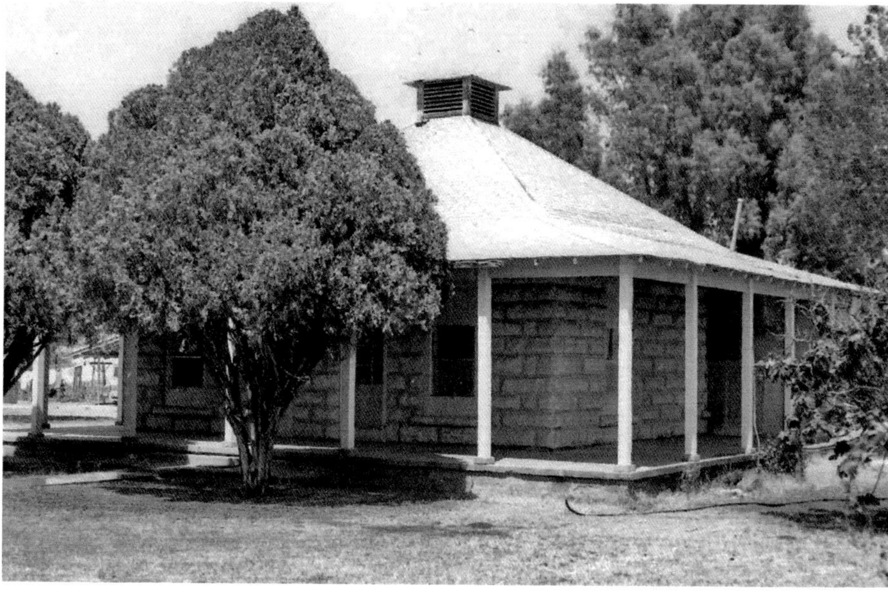

The Teacherage.

"Well, you know, Sonja, I can't afford to be in the business of historic preservation! I've got a reservation to run."

I pestered the superintendent for several weeks, and finally, as the judge in the Gospel of Luke who became sick and tired of the old widow's nagging, he let me have my way. I even convinced him to leave the guesthouse behind the big house, although he had been adamant about that not being part of the deal.

"The guesthouse really does have to go," he'd said. "It's got termites."

"Oh, I *really* want the guesthouse!" I'd begged, not caring about termites.

Most government quarters, of course, don't have "guesthouses," and the small adobe building with authentic wooden vigas holding up the roof had not been intended as such. Used originally as an activity center for the public school, the two small meeting rooms had evolved over the years into bedrooms, and someone had eventually tacked on a primitive bathroom. It seemed almost like a playhouse, and I knew it would be a wonderful place to put up the dozens of visitors who came our way.

"I could do so much with it," I promised him.

He sighed and told me he would call an exterminator.

Joe Haught, the plant management chief who, with his wife, Elma, had raised his own children in the house, brought us a wooden glider swing and hung it from the ceiling of the north veranda. It was from Joe and Elma we learned the house's history.

The house had a name, the only house I ever lived in that did. It was called the Teacherage, and it was a genuine Arizona Territorial, built in 1910, two years before statehood, by the Apache Manuel Victor, who, at the age of one hundred, told Richard about the days when eagles flew over Salt River Canyon.

Joe told us the Teacherage had been the first San Carlos schoolhouse. A wall had originally separated what were now the living and dining rooms, with the classroom on one side and the teachers' living quarters on the other.

The original part of the house was square, with doors but no hallways. A large bedroom was behind the living room, the kitchen was behind the dining room and a bathroom was between the bedroom and kitchen. Two additional bedrooms and a laundry room had been built at the back when the BIA took over the house to use as government quarters. The south windows of the house looked out on the walled friary of the Catholic mission, the north windows on the wide, dirt turnaround driveway we shared with our neighbors. In the middle of the driveway stood a tall, old mesquite tree and a large prickly pear cactus that bore the beautiful fuchsia fruit Apaches loved.

"This old house had bats," Elma told us. "Acres and acres of 'em. And if you've never taken on an attic full of bats, you've just no idea how hard it is to get rid of 'em."

"They'd congregated up there because it was dark and quiet," Joe said, "but at night after we'd go to bed, they'd come a swoopin' down over our heads. One night when they were all down there flyin' around, we suddenly decided to turn on the lights and drive 'em outside."

"Seemed like it took us hours," Elma said. "We were chasin' 'em around with a broom and a mop."

"And it was July and so damned hot," Joe said, "that all I had on was my boxer shorts, and Elma was wearin' her little short flimsy nightgown. We attracted quite a sizeable crowd outside, let me tell you, laughin' at us through the open door and windows."

The day we moved into the Teacherage, I walked slowly through each room, marveling at the hardwood floors, the walls two feet thick, the tall, deep windows. But most of all, I was struck by the two old five-sconce chandeliers that illuminated the living and dining rooms. Those chandeliers seemed, from the first time I saw them hanging thirteen feet above me, to be more than accessories or functional ornaments. As we settled into our new home, those chandeliers shone down on everything we brought to the rooms, made them fit together and blend in a new way: the Apache and Pima baskets, the Navajo rugs, the pine church pew from the mission next door, the old round mahogany dining table, the clay pots of cacti and geraniums on the window ledges. I began to think of the chandeliers as the soul of the house. I came to love them even more during the day when they were not turned on. They looked so beautifully dark and primitive against the white ceilings that, when evening came, I longed to see them lighted by candles instead of electricity. What lovely flickering shadows they would have thrown around those walls!

From the front edge of the veranda of the west porch, directly over the top step, we hung—purely for decoration—an old iron bell we had found in Mexico. To our surprise, our Apache friends, instead of pushing the electric buzzer next to the front door, rang this bell and waited for us to come to them on the veranda steps. Was this in keeping with their custom of approaching a house discreetly? I think it was. They rang the bell only one time; they never jingled it, so that whenever we heard that one lovely chime we knew we had Indian visitors.

On one of our first nights in the Teacherage, we awakened after midnight to the sound of horseshoes clopping on the veranda. Through our open bedroom window we saw Rambler, the large gentle horse that roamed around town like a stray dog. Moonlight streamed down on him, turning his dark coat silver. Behind him the mesquite tree shimmered with a numinous radiance. We drifted back to sleep while Rambler stood watch. When we awoke in the morning he was gone, and the mesquite tree was back to its normal greenish gray.

I loved to smell that mesquite tree early in the morning after a rain. I would bring a cup of coffee back to bed and sit there for half an hour or so, watching, listening, thinking. There was nothing else in that room, no pictures, no decorations of any kind, no furniture other than the bed and an antique highboy—just those white walls and, directly across from the bed, that tall, deep window framing the tree.

Sometimes when I was alone in the house I thought I would hear a door close. Oddly, I was never frightened, even though I had always been afraid of strange sounds, afraid of the dark. Perhaps I so loved living in those layers of history that there was no room for fear. I did wonder, once, if the Teacherage might be haunted, but I quickly dismissed the thought. Had that house been haunted, the Apaches would have known—they knew that kind of thing better than anyone—and they would never have entered the place. As with their Navajo cousins, the one thing they would not abide was a ghost. Chiliboy, especially, was adamant about ghosts, and he came to our house every Wednesday evening to practice the music for the Sunday Mass.

The antique plumbing, cooling and heating, which broke down frequently, did not worry us because we ourselves never had to repair them. Almost as soon as Richard called Joe to report a busted cooler or a leaky toilet, our old friends Raleigh and Ralph would bang on our front door (no bell for them) and announce they'd arrived to fix things up. I was always happy to see them—not only for the repairs but also for the laughter.

"Hey, Richard, how's the weather down there?" Raleigh once yelled from the top of the perilously peaked roof where he was repairing the swamp cooler. His voice boomed through the vents and into the bathroom, startling Richard, who was home on his lunch break.

"I couldn't figure out where Raleigh was," Richard told me later. "Here was this disembodied voice floating in from the pipes or somewhere. For a second I was sure *Candid Camera* had caught me in an awkward position."

ONE DAY, WHEN NOELLE was four years old (and speaking English with an Apache accent), she made Benjamin Patten come into the house with the sandwich I had given him at the front door.

"*Dahindah!*" she commanded, leading him by the hand.

"You bossy, *na'ilihn*," Benjamin complained. You bossy, girl. He appealed to me with bleary eyes.

I stared at my daughter as she tugged him along.

"*Dahindah!*" she said again. Sit down. She pointed to one of the bentwood chairs at the table.

"I think Benjamin wants to go outside," I told Noelle.

"Oh, nooooo," she said, exhaling the end of the word exactly the way Linda did. "She wanna stay ina house."

"He," I corrected her. "Not she." I sighed. Would my daughter, like some Apaches, have trouble with pronouns for the rest of her life?

A house that has sheltered many generations forms its own unique character, and the Teacherage was no exception. The old medicine man Britton Goode told Richard that many years ago, he had heard his first radio broadcast in what was now our dining room. I often thought of that as our family sat around the dining room table. I thought about the children who had gone to school here, about the other people who had lived here or who, like Britton, kept happy memories of the house.

Not only was it the oldest house we'd ever lived in, it was the happiest place of our married life. It possessed us with its spirit and became a refuge,

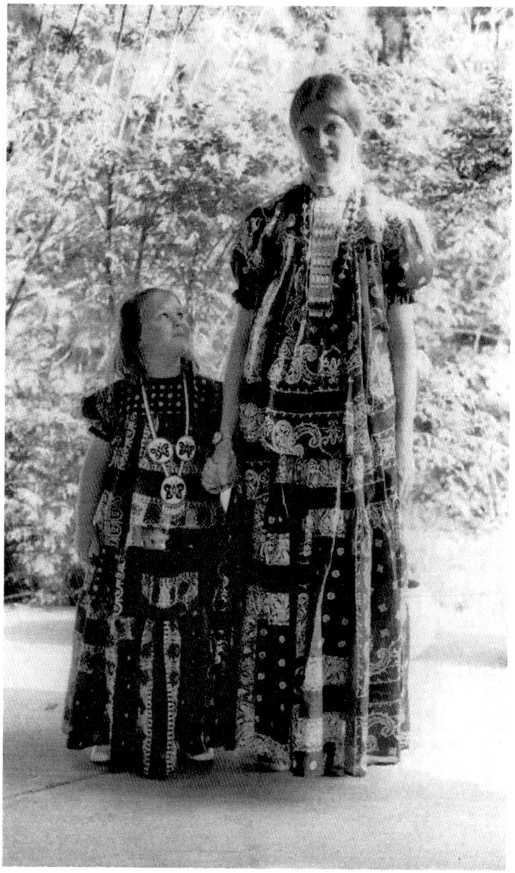

Noelle and I, wearing our Apache camp dresses, stand on the veranda of the Teacherage.

generous and openhearted, to all who rang the bell. Celebrations abounded.

"If you aren't ending one party you're starting another," Father Bart told us one evening when he'd come to our house to dinner. "You have the gift of hospitality."

"It's the house," I said. "Things just happen here." It was so easy, so natural, to create festivities in our home: birthdays and wedding anniversaries, First Communions, St. Patrick's Day, the Feast of Guadalupe…

But it had not always been this way. The first Thanksgiving we lived in the Teacherage, we gave a dinner and nobody came. While the turkey cooled in the kitchen we waited for Linda and Ambrose, for Raleigh and Joanne and their children.

"Hey, Mom, when do we get to eat?" Patrick asked. Christopher patted the turkey and sighed. When Joanne rang the bell on the veranda we all perked up, but when Richard opened the door she thrust a note into his hand and ran back to her car.

"We won't be able to make it to your house tonight," Richard read. "Raleigh has disappeared. I am sorry but thanks for the invitation."

What happened to our guests? Linda and Ambrose visited us so often, unannounced; why did they not come when they were invited? They never gave us any explanation, and we could never bring ourselves to ask. Nor did I mention anything to Raleigh when he appeared the following week, joking and teasing as usual, to repair the heating unit. Some barriers, we learned, would take a long time to cross.

It took only until two weeks after Easter. We asked Father Bart to say Mass at the Teacherage before a potluck in our backyard, and we invited everyone we knew. To our amazement, everyone showed up—even some people we didn't know. But the wedding was the biggest and most successful celebration of all. When Nancy Chase, the white schoolteacher who had grown up in San Carlos, got married in the Catholic mission, most of the town came to the reception. People swarmed through our house and out onto the veranda. The newly elected tribal chairman himself toasted the bride and groom.

The guesthouse was often full, just as I had known it would be. On holidays we always had our mothers and Richard's stepfather and grandmother from Phoenix and, during the summers, friends from Vermont, California, Chicago and Boston. John and Terri brought our godson Denis along with a five-pound hunk of cheese and a gallon of wine. They fell in love with the guesthouse the minute they walked in the door. It was romantic, they said.

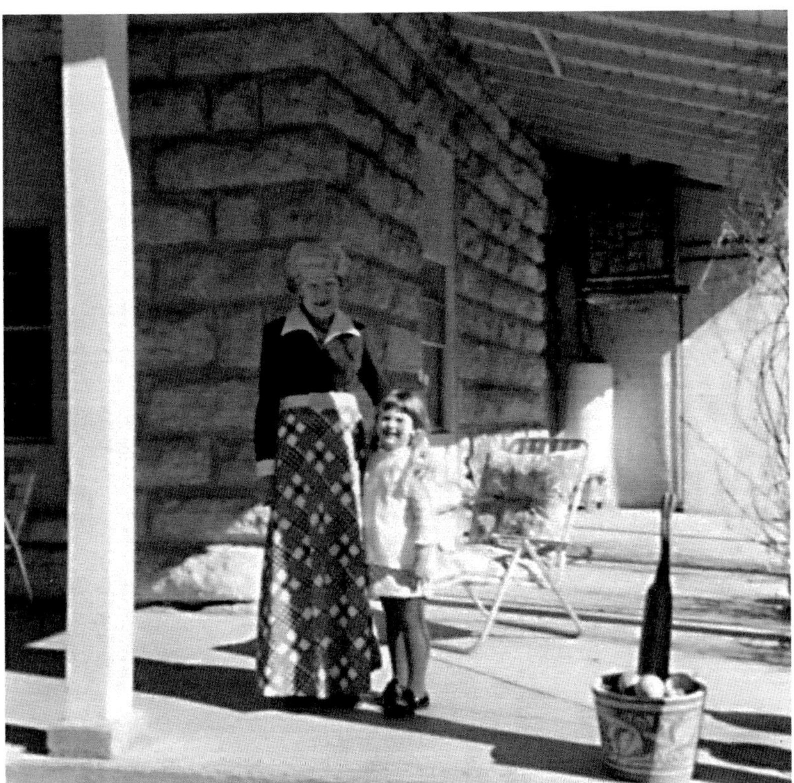

Richard's grandmother, Jennie, with Noelle, on the veranda of the Teacherage.

And one Easter we were so crowded after we'd installed Laurel, her two daughters and our godson Adam out in back, my mother in the sofa bed in the living room and Billy Otwell in a sleeping bag on the hardwood floor of the dining room that Richard's family took refuge in a motel in Globe.

Billy, who was an architectural student at Arizona State, brought a giant wooden cable spool he had salvaged from the telephone company, and all of the kids from the neighborhood practiced rolling on it. Turning the spool on its side, they balanced on top—a scary seven feet from the ground—and propelled the enormous wheel wildly across the lawn.

The old house came into its own, most of all, at Christmas. When my mother, who'd been born in 1899, walked in the door the first year we lived there, she stopped, suddenly, and looked around.

"Your home reminds me of when I was a very little girl," she said, her eyes lingering on Ambrose's Scotch pine tree, which reached to the ceiling, our silver wedding pitcher filled with live holly, the antique secretary with the face of the Old North Wind carved into the top and her own baby grand piano in the corner. "It takes me back nearly seventy years."

Behind her, my honorary Aunt Tad carried an oddly shaped thing sticking out of white tissue paper.

"Now, your mother *swore* you'd rather have this than something I just went out and bought," Aunt Tad said, her hearty laugh filling the room. "I'm afraid I didn't wrap it very well."

I ripped the paper from a fine old brass candelabrum with four arms and a center holder.

"It was on my mother's dining room sideboard when I was a child," Aunt Tad told me as I threw my arms around her. "And now it looks as if it's come home again," she said when I placed the candelabrum in the middle of the mahogany table. "I swear it does!"

When Joan and Arnie Gass arrived from San Diego and placed a menorah next to the brass candelabrum, I was struck by the gifts of light we'd been given that day. And in the evening as the candelabrum and the menorah blazed before me and the chandeliers above me, I looked around the table at the friends and relatives who had joined us for Christmas dinner and I felt absolutely rooted and at peace.

"Nothing is ever lost," another dear old aunt who possessed a definite mystical streak once told me firmly the first time she saw my home.

"Nothing," my mother agreed.

I hoped Aunt Ione and Mother were right, but I doubted it the day Richard was promoted to another federal agency in Denver. Pregnant with our fourth child, I saw my dream of the christening party I had envisioned in this house of light fade away. Sadly, I walked around my home alone, after all the furniture had been taken to the moving van, and said goodbye.

We were the last family to live in the Teacherage. The first time I returned to San Carlos for a visit, I discovered my house had been converted back into a schoolroom. The walls had been freshly painted white, and children's desks stood in a line across the living and dining room floors. The fine old dwelling had come full circle.

The Teacherage is gone now, a victim, finally, of a bureaucracy "not in the business of historic preservation." The last time I saw my home, before it was demolished, its windows were smashed and its walls covered with graffiti. Broken wires dangled from the ceiling where my beloved old chandeliers once hung. I thought my heart would break.

"Poor old house," our daughter Holly whispered when she saw, for the only time, the place of her conception. And Patrick, by this time a medical student sponsored by the Indian Health Service, quickly turned his face away.

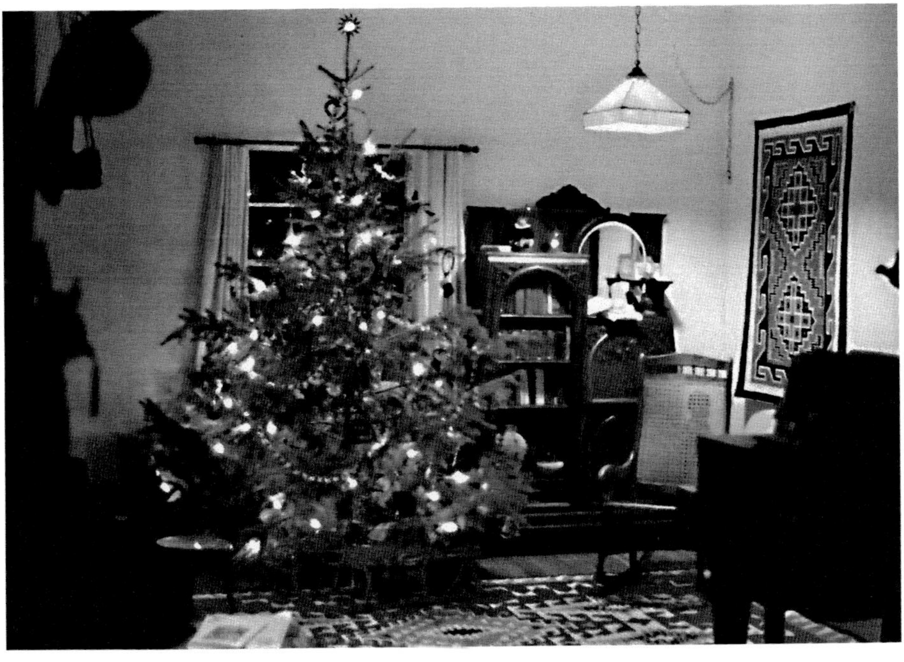

The Teacherage on Christmas Eve with the Scotch pine Ambrose cut on the northern part of the reservation.

A few years later, I received a letter from Joe Haught, the old plant management chief, from his retirement home in New Mexico. He apologized for the typographical errors, which he explained were the result of his deteriorating vision. "If you ever come our way," he'd typed, "I've got something for you."

The following summer when Richard and I drove back to Denver from Phoenix, we stopped in Albuquerque. It was the first time we'd seen Joe and Elma in years. Joe was nearly blind. We talked over the San Carlos days for a while and then Joe, groping his way along a wall, led us to the garage. I felt sad, but also curious, as he fumbled around in a large cardboard box and threw crumpled newspaper onto the floor. Suddenly, he grinned. I stared at Joe, and tears stung my eyes when I saw what he held in each hand. They were grimy and spattered with white paint, but I recognized them. They were the chandeliers—my chandeliers!—that once blazed at weddings and Easters and the most wonderful Christmases of my life.

"I saved 'em for you," Joe said. "I always knew you liked 'em."

You saved more than chandeliers, I thought but could not say. My aunt and mother had been right. Nothing is ever lost. I believed them.

THE SAN CARLOS APACHE TRIBE

P.O. BOX O
SAN CARLOS, ARIZONA 85550

(602) 475-2372

Buck Kitcheyan
Chairman
San Carlos Apache Tribe

April 6, 1975

Mr. Richard David
P. O. Box 254
San Carlos, Arizona

Dear Mr. David:

For many of us here on the San Carlos Apache Indian Reservation, your departure to Denver for a new job is an occasion mixed with joy and sadness. Joy, because we share with you the opportunity for new challenges, a well-deserved promotion and a better climate! Sadness, because we will miss your services as one BIA employee and friend to whom we could turn for assistance with trust and confidence; and sadness, because we do not like to see a very close friend leave a part of our daily lives. Let it not be said that Apaches are without emotion.

Perhaps many others will not agree with what we say on behalf of you and your family, but our own individual feelings do run deep, because we do know of your many accomplishments and unselfish efforts to help the needy and unfortunate members of our Apache tribe -- oftentimes beyond the call of duty and even when such efforts were at your own expense. We know also that in all of your endeavors on behalf of our tribal members, your intentions were always good and that you tried your best. In this respect, I think we can say that your own parents and family taught you well and should be very proud of you for your work and cooperation with our tribe.

As you may know, some of us view the departure of members of our tribe for parts unknown as a departure of members and relatives of our own respective families. Thus, we view such an invaluable loss as a personal loss of our own natural resource. It is with this perspective, therefore, that we would like you to know that we will miss you and your family. And if there was ever a moment in our lives when we could humble ourselves to help one another, it could well be on certain occasions such as this when we honor or pay tribute to such people as you and your family; when selfishness is discouraged; when spiritual attributes abound, and in an atmosphere when a Supreme Being is accepted.

I think all of this symbolizes the essence of brotherly love but my own thought is that this could well mean the substance of Apache unity when all of the individuals of our tribe come together. May you be blessed for helping to refresh our memories and for being around to elicit these truths.

Respectfully yours,

Tony Machukay

Tony Machukay, Member
Tribal Council
San Carlos Apache Tribe

Farewell letter from the tribal council.

About the Author

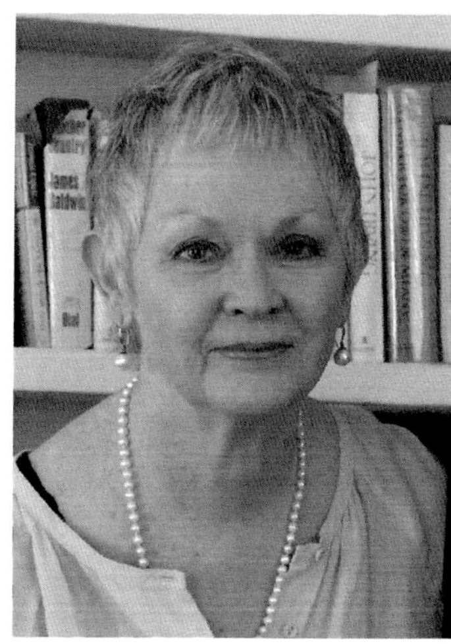

Sonja White David has published book reviews in the *Denver Post* and feature articles in *Denver Magazine* and *Bloomsbury Review*. She is the author of *Lady Law: The Story of Arizona Supreme Court Justice Lorna Lockwood*. *Apache Sunrise: Memories from San Carlos* is her second book.

A longtime Red Cross water safety instructor with additional certification in adapted aquatics, Sonja established, at the request of the City of Lakewood, Colorado, a one-on-one swim program for people with special needs, for which she recruited volunteers from local high schools and service clubs.

One of her own favorite volunteer activities was with Project Renumber at the Denver Art Museum, where, for several hours each week for a year, she painted tiny numbers from the international museum system on each Apache basket in the archives.

In 1981, she received a grant to attend the Bennington Writers' Workshop in Vermont, and in 1982, she was one of ten writers and artists inducted into the Rocky Mountain Women's Institute in Denver. A graduate of Arizona State University, she was awarded, in 1995, a master of arts in theology, *summa cum laude*, from St. Thomas Theological Seminary in Denver.

Married to Richard for fifty-four years, Sonja has four children, six grandchildren and a calico cat named Princess Grace. Her work in progress, *Pilgrim Heart*, is a memoir of pilgrimages made to usual and unusual sites.